Rediscover Your Greatness

A Guide to an INSPIRED and FULFILLED Life

Dr. Vic Manzo Jr.
Co-Founder of The Wellness Path
Founder of Empower Your Reality

**EMPOWER
YOUR REALITY**
Discover - Expand - Evolve

Sign up today to get exclusive access to Dr. Vic's most up to date podcast episodes, Vlogs, online programs, workshops, books, seminars and more.

Visit us online at **www.EmpowerYourReality.com**
Subscribe to Dr. Vic's Podcast:
www.TheMindfulExperiment.com

Mention of specific companies, organizations, or authorities in this book does not imply endorsement by the author or publisher, nor does mention of specific companies, organizations, or authorities imply that they endorse this book, its author or the publisher.

Internet addresses given in this book were accurate at the time it went to press.

© 2018 by Dr. Victor Manzo Jr.

All rights reserved. No part of this publication may be reproduced or transmitted in ay form or by any means, electronic or mechanical, including photocopying, recording, or any other information storage and retrieval system, without the written permission of the publisher, Empower Your Reality.

Printed in the United States of America

ISBN-13: 978-1-7321866-3-7
ISBN-10: 1-7321866-3-4

To the vision of an enlightened society to where we realize the potential of who we are and experience it on a daily basis. May the higher vibrational consciousness raise the overall level of the human collective, to experience a more fulfilled and inspired life...

Book has been written in memory of my grandmother. She passed away during the time of being published. Until we meet again Nonna...

DEDICATION

First and foremost, I want to thank my beautiful and amazing wife. She has chosen me to be a part of her life. She is my rock and my voice of reason. Thank you for always being there for me with love, encouragement and support.

My parents for truly working so hard to give us a better life. It is because of your hard work, it gave me the opportunity to be where I am today. I could never accomplished all I did without you both!

To my friends, family and extended tribe, you all have helped me in the journey of being who I am today. Thank you!

To my grandparents. Thank you for always sharing your unconditional love and being a light within my life. You are deeply missed.

To my practice members for allowing me to be a part of their journey in their life. It truly is an honor.

Table of Contents

Introduction……………………………………….. Pg. 6

Ch. 1- Essence Of Who You Are………………… Pg. 8

Ch. 2 - Focusing On Source Energy……………… Pg. 33

Ch. 3 - Words Are The Fabric……………………. Pg. 54

Ch. 4 - We Are All Interdependent………………. Pg. 72

Ch. 5 - Free Will Is Your Spiritual Birthright……….. Pg. 90

Ch. 6 - We Are Positive And Negative…………... Pg. 110

Ch. 7 - Biggest Interference Of Life………………. Pg. 124

Ch. 8 - Language Of The Universe……………... Pg. 143

Ch. 9 - Our Mind Contains Limited Info……………. Pg. 157

Ch. 10 - The Inevitable Truth……………………... Pg. 168

Ch. 11 - Creating An Inspired And Fulfilled Life...… Pg. 181

Introduction

The journey of life is truly an unique experience for anyone to embark. To come from bliss, peace and unconditional love and forget who you are to enjoy a human experience is one brave thing any one of us souls can do but we do it. Why? What is the purpose? Why am I here at this time? What is my potential? How do I achieve a more fulfilled and inspired life?

This book will help you answer these questions and much more. The main purpose of this book is designed to help you rediscover your greatness but at the same token, how you can express that to your fullest. It is understanding the fabric of your reality and how do you transform your life with some basic principles.

Truth be told, you are a creator. You are the artist of your life. You are the author. You are the producer of your movie. You are the star of the movie. You are the writer of the movie. You are orchestrator and the musicians of your own symphony. Everything happens in your life because of you. The Universe is always working FOR you.

At the age of 34 years old, I decided to write this book because I was tired of seeing individuals suffer on levels that they were creating but felt that, it was the life they chose. As if, they didn't have the power to change things. And for those who were wanting to change things but always ended up meeting a dead end, this book will give you the tools you to need to find your path and your journey in whatever way you choose.

I will be sharing personal stories, concepts, principles, universal laws and sharing my heart with you in this book. My goal of this book is to truly help you rediscover who you are. You have greatness within you and the power that exists within, humanity will never be able to measure. It is infinite potential and my goal is to help you know where to look and help express that to the world.

If you are here at this time in this world, know we are living in blessed times. It is a miracle that you exist. I heard Gary

Vaynerchuk state in a talk, "The odds of you being a human being is 1 out of 400 trillion." Think about that for a second. 1 out of 400 trillion. But yet, you are here. You are reading this book, at this evolutionary time in the life of Earth's existence. It is truly a blessing to be here and now.

As we go through the work of this book, my goal is for you to truly keep an open mind and work with what is shared. Everything that I share in this book truly has transformed my life for the better. I see every aspect of life in a different perspective and truly welcome my challenges and my failures because it is what helps me evolve into who I desire to BE. Growth cannot exist without a challenge and in order to continue growing in your life, you must face your challenges and accept your failures. The greatest lesson I have learned in life is, my greatest moments of growth and success has all come from my failures.

May this book truly help you create a fulfilled and inspired life for the rest of your life so you may live and realize your greatness!

I am excited you are here.

Dr. Vic Manzo Jr.

Chapter 1

The Essence of Who You Are

Mastering others is STRENGTH. Mastering yourself is TRUE POWER.

Loa Tzu

Who we are, is a big question that has long been asked. It has been asked for eons, and for most people, the best idea someone has of who they are is based upon a label or title. This label or title is something determined by the profession you are in, the things you do, the people you love or the 193 variety of labels we title ourselves with. But the deeper question I seek for you to ask is, are you truly this label? Are you what makes up this label?

The goal of this chapter is to truly give you a deep insight, a breakdown of the fabric of who you really are because once you're able to answer the question of who you really are, infinite potential can exist. By the time you know who you really are, you'll experience freedom, and that is when you can expand, grow and evolve to the person you want to become or experience. So, let's jump fully in, and not just test the waters, as we embark on a REDISCOVERY of who you really are.

Let us connect back to when you were a child. During that time, you innately knew who you were. Just take a moment and look at children and at the AW of life that they live by. Remember when you used to get excited about the simple things in life? If you've forgotten this, don't worry. One of my goals of writing this book is to help bring that back. And if you are the person who already remembers this, my goal is to add more fuel to the fire. Expand and empower the reality you have created already. When we were children, we lived in the moment and always took everything as new. You had curiosity! Curiosity is what keeps us young. We are curious, ask questions and seem to be amazed by the AW and miracle of life. Kids are always curious about everything. Take a look at a 1- to 2-year-old and watch how they can do the same thing over and over and enjoy that process.

Sometimes, you see a child just rotate and stare at a pencil for 30 minutes. How about movies? Do you remember as a kid how you can watch your favorite movie over and over and over again? But as an adult, you cannot do that? Kids can watch the same movie ten times in a day and never get bored. Why is that?

To a child, this is perfectly normal and fine. But the question I ask is, "when did the switch happen?"

You see, as we get to the age of around 7 years old, things start to change for children. They are taught logic, fear, worry, and many other things. It has been said that children come into this world perfect and the adults damage them. I know this is a strong statement, but the thing is, as adults/parents, we share our fears, worries and experiences with children, which makes them to start developing similar fears, worries and belief systems.

As the age of 7 hits, we start to develop the conditioning of the world of where humanity is at. It is then we start to take in the level of consciousness of what the world is experiencing. Let me dive deeper into this.

What happens then is, we start to lose our curiosity of life. We start to lose that AW feeling of amazement. We start to stop being in the present moment and start focusing on things of the future or the past. We start to dislike something like school, and just focus on what we would do after school and just can't wait for that to happen.

Let us say the opposite happens and we didn't do well on a quiz. We start to worry about the quiz and how we are not doing well in school. It is bad enough you are already feeling bad about it, but now you have to hear your parents talk to you about how you need to pick up your grades and do well in school. All this does, is build the pressure and stress upon you.

The more this cycle happens, the farther and farther we disconnect from who we really are. And before you know it, we are so far disconnected to the extent that we don't remember what it is like. We see a child and go, how lucky for them. They live in a world that is AW and they are happy about everything. I cannot be that way. This doesn't exist for me and you go down the whole shopping list of excuses of why this isn't.

The biggest reason is due to the titles and labels that you allowed to be you. What you accepted as your identity. Now you let the labels create your identity. This all starts with the addition of titles.

When we were a baby, all we were, was a son or a daughter. You can add niece/nephew and a cousin also. But that's it. Nothing else. Life was simple and easy. All you needed to fulfill was the role of being a baby, BUT as time passed by, things changed and more titles started to be created. As you created more titles, it was your unconscious way of stating, this is who I am.

For example, I am a chiropractor. As a chiropractor, there are a construct of ideas that humanity views a chiropractor as. Chiropractors, think a specific way for the most part. We have a way of living, ideas, belief systems and more. One of the statements that Chiropractors all agree upon is that the body is a self-healing, self-regulating organism. A chiropractor is going to focus on an individual's nervous system and make sure that it is free of any nerve interference from the brain and body connection. Our life is constructed around what our title is. These labels and titles are what construct our thinking and actually limit us in more ways than one, which we have allowed.

Another example would be stating I am a democrat or a republican. You can look and say, "Well, what type of democrat/republican are you?" When you start to look at this, you would see how I think, act, behave, belief systems and more just from this label. And from this label, this is what you would commonly see and experience, and unconsciously, you take that on as your reality. This is my way of life because this is what a republican or democrat should be.

The "should" part is the belief system of society of what you allowed into your mind to believe.

This concept also works very well with Religions. If you are a Christian, you believe, act, and live a specific way. If you are a Catholic, Buddhist, Muslim, Jewish, etc., all these constructs come in and actually limit you. I have said for years, being raised Italian Roman-Catholic, that these are things that can guide you in your life, but it is not who you truly are. Because your true source is not bound to any of these ideals. Not to any religion or belief system.

My goal in this entire book is for you to realize the TRUTH of who you are or understand a deeper layer to the fabric of who you are.

Labels and titles are just something that limits the light of who you truly are.

Labels and titles are just a program, a conditioning. It is a way to have you believe you are living your life and being free, but in truth, you are living to ideals of whoever it is that has accepted X, Y, Z to be this way.

For example, being a Chiropractor, in my business, I should act a specific way, talk a specific way, have a specific office, tables, etc. It is what the majority of chiropractors do, and so, I believe this is what I should do also. I've been told by very successful chiropractors, the ways to run a successful office and to do certain types of things. The question is, am I showing who I really am in the process or am I just following a method of what the title states I should be?

How many times in our lives do we follow the same thing? Since I am X, and all individuals who are X, act, live, think and be this way? How much of that is a program, a conditioning, and not truly showing you who you are?

All these things are programs and conditioning that you have accepted to be the TRUTH. And since you have accepted it to be the TRUTH, your reality will show just that. You see, all of this is just a program. It is a conditioning. The more times you see something showing up in your life, the more you will believe it to be true. Welcome to the model of MSM to a specific degree.

If you tell a lie loud enough and long enough, people will start to believe you. Adolf Hitler.

So, when you start to look at your titles and labels that we all put on ourselves, what we truly are doing is putting filters, blinders or creating tunnel vision for your life. We are closing other possibilities out and just focusing on what it is we are and how we live our life in this fashion. Eventually, we believe and allow for this to dictate our life rather than be who we truly are. This starts to develop the conditioning and programming to have you see your life in a specific way and start to only experience this one way rather than any other way that exists.

One thing I like to make clear though is, there is nothing wrong with utilizing a specific religion, specific profession and so forth. The truth behind all of this is to have you realize, it is OK to have labels, but don't let the labels define who you are. Don't let the labels become your belief system and expectations of life. Too many times, we allow for these labels and titles to dictate our lives.

So, the question then is, if we strip all our labels, titles, experiences, belief systems and every fabric that makes up our identity right now, who are we?

This is a heavy question I ask for you to take time with. Look at yourself in the mirror and ask yourself, "Who really am I?" Who is the person who observes all the thoughts? Who is the person who is observing all the information that is coming into the brain?

When you look in the mirror, you see your physical self. But your physical self is not you. Who is the person, looking at the person is where the truth of who you are starts to uncover.

When you look at your body, it is like being in your car, looking at the outside of the car. When you are in the car, you can look on the inside, but are you the car? No. You are experiencing what it is like to be in a car, drive the car, experience all that is possible for this one car to experience. But, at the end of the day, you are not the car.

Now, let's look at all the cars that have ever existed in the past 50 years. When you think about that, there are a ton of different cars out there. As the cars have evolved, so have the experiences. 50 years ago, they didn't have traction control sensors on the cars. They didn't have navigation systems. They didn't have satellite radio, driver's lane assistant and all the wonderful technological features cars have today.

You see, one car, at one moment, is an experience, but after a period of time, this is only one car. How many cars and how many experiences can you have from all the cars that exist at the different timelines that they existed on? It starts to get infinite because once you start adding geographical locations to the mix and different timelines, it starts to get more and more complex.

So, this car (your body) is the experience you are enjoying at this time. But in no way, are you the label of it. It is like saying you are a Ford F150 (love these trucks) or a Maserati or Jaguar, Toyota, etc. You limit your experience and think this is all that you experience based upon the label that was put on you.

Another example of how labels define your life. I was born and raised in a small Italian community. My father was born in Italy and my mom is a 1st generation Italian. I was raised by my parents in a very Italian way with my maternal grandparents adding to the Italian within me. Growing up, I thought all people acted similar to the experiences of what I had experienced in my life. Italian people are very passionate and can be very passionate about everything and this can lead to very heated arguments or conversations quickly. Sometimes, even overreacting can occur and I would experience these things and think this is how the world was.

As I continued to live in this type of atmosphere until I went away to college, it was then I experienced a whole new world I never knew existed. I started to see how vastly different human beings can be, but also saw the similarities. It started to teach me how, our minds, are just programs, a conditioning. And what you feed it, it becomes. All my life (19 years), I thought life and human beings acted and behaved in the ways I experienced because I accepted that life was X. But, what I learned overtime is that, it was just what I was experiencing. It was only one way of the infinite ways of how life is.

This led me to realize, the shift you want to experience in your life has to happen between the ears. I started to see this more and more in my own chiropractic office. If I was able to help patients see life in a different perspective and slowly help re-wire their brain into a new perspective, they would have an entirely different experience. And, the practice members that I have had the privilege to work with and help in this fashion have been mind-blown to see the results that have come out of this, in their own life and in their health.

After years of practicing, this concept kept coming back to me to share this message with the world. And this message is, starting to realize who you really are and rediscover your greatness, but more importantly, rediscover the laws that govern this world and how you can use them to create the life you desire.

You see, most people focus on the negative. I ask my practice members, what is good today on basically, every single visit, to help break this pattern. We are so focused on what is wrong instead of focusing on what is right with our lives.

Why I do this is because, it is a miracle to be alive right now, reading this book. How everything has orchestrated in your life to line up to this, is just impossible, but it is happening.

Don't believe me…. Well, let us ask the top leading scientists at CERN (Council of European Nuclear Research) that were baffled with new findings that were showing them, it is impossible for the Universe to exist BUT it does! How? How is this possible? Again, it is the miracle of life and how life just manages to defy all odds to evolve, grow and expand.

Heck, the wisdom within your body within one given second is more wisdom on health than all the great minds that have ever walked this planet put together. Talk about unbelievable.

I digress.

Alright, let us discuss the concept of your left brain always analyzing to help you in this lifetime. You see, our left brain is the one which will set a goal and tell us, here are the steps and ways to achieve it. Ever heard the quote, "When you create a plan, God laughs at you?" There is much truth to this.

Your left brain is what creates more and more labels. When we look at the left brain, it is all about breaking things down into very logical concepts. For example, look at how many different type of Christianity Religions exist. Based on www.answers.com, there are 29 different ones. And all of these have a slightly different belief system than the other.

When we look at the different types of democrats or republicans that exist, the list is extensive. When we look at the different types of medical doctors, the list is extensive. When we look at the different types of screens, desks, computers, books, etc., the list is extensive.

I am not saying this is a bad thing. The reason why I bring this is up is to show how much we label, break down and want to put a label on things. Humans love to label things.

But what if, when we label something, it loses its magic? This is what I was trying to share with you earlier. When you put a label on something, or on yourself, you start to limit who you are. You start the journey of losing the TRUTH of your source.
What pains me the most in this world right now is all the children who are given labels and believe in them. These labels are Autism, ADHD, Allergies, Asthma, Sensory Processing and much

more. When you give a child this label and they believe in it, they accept the path of what this experience will be and who knows, if they will ever challenge it.

Let me share a quick personal story. My first 5 years of experiencing being human was not something I wish upon anyone. Being pulled out of my mom's birth canal that created ligament damage in my neck, skull issues and much more. Due to being born with bilateral club foot, I needed to wear a cast on my left foot to hopefully straighten it out and perform exercise on my right. Every single night, my mother had to strap me into braces to help my legs straighten out with a bar that would put my feet in a specific position. Long story short, at the age of 7 years old, I had a medical doctor tell me that there was something wrong with my left hip, and that due to the severity of it, I would not be able to play any sports in high school at all and by the age of 30, I would need a full hip replacement.

Now, my question to you is, do you believe this or do you challenge to see if this is true? When you put a label on yourself, are you living in this program/conditioning just like the medical doctor told me what I was going to experience, or are you going to challenge, go outside your comfort zone and see what may be possible?

Remember one thing about life. You are the producer, the actor, writer, star of the show and everything that makes the show. You have the power to choose what reality you want to experience and at the age of 7, I believed I could experience something different.

I remember coming home that day, sad, upset, crying and just in disbelief. Then, I said, no one tells me no except me. And I let this be a way of how I live. And I said, I will play sports and prove these doctors wrong. Long story short, when I entered high school, I played 2 sports (baseball and soccer), and outside of school, I played tackle football with friends almost every weekend, basketball and racquetball 3-4 days a week plus workout. And I continued to do this even till when I reached the age of 17 and I was playing baseball for my high school and ended up playing on the weekends for another 1-2 teams on top of everything else. I loved sports and I allowed for that to drive me to prove to myself that it was possible and I achieved that.

As I am writing this book, at the age of 34, I can attest that my hips are clean, healthy joints with no signs of degeneration or arthritis nor do I need any signs of hip surgery at all.

Never let someone else or a label tell you how your experience should be in life. We are living in a time that it is so essential for us to live our truth. To live our life the way we want to and break out of these prisons that we have created for ourselves.

All these labels, belief systems and so much more that hold us down from experiencing life at our fullest and realizing our true potential, is what this book is all about.

We talked about how we label ourselves, but let's dive into who we truly are and this process is more of a rediscovery rather than learning something new. And I wanted to start by sharing a story that started me on this journey…

I was born and raised in a small town in Illinois that was, at the time, highly populated with Italians. As being raised an Italian Roman Catholic, I attended church weekly with my mother and/or grandparents. I remember becoming an altar boy because that is what a good boy would do. I even took it as far as becoming an Eucharist minister. I remember reading the Bible twice. I was told that most great knowledge comes from the Bible, and being a Catholic, all I ever needed to know was in the Bible.

As I dived deeper and deeper into my religion, I started to have more and more questions. More things started to not make sense. If we only had one life and this one life is all we have, this seems to be a lot of pressure. I wanted answers to all the questions I had, but when I asked, I didn't get a response that felt right within myself. It didn't fulfill the deep seeking I had within.

As I continued to seek answers of the Truth because my philosophy that I live by is, everything in life has to be challenged at some point or another. That way, you keep things fresh and make sure that if a model or system is not working, you can grow, expand and evolve into new things to make sure you are always growing, evolving and expanding to the life you desire.

As time went on, I was asking friends, priest, Christians and many other forms of Christianity to see who could share some light on these questions I had. And the deeper I went, the more confusing and vastly different the answers were.

You see, when you find truth, regardless of anything, the truth will shine through time. For example, in Chiropractic, we have known for the past 123 years that Chiropractic has existed, the truth is still the same: The body is a self-healing and self-organizing organism. All Chiropractors work on the nervous system to help improve the self-healing and self-regulating systems of the human body. When you have no interference within your nervous system, it is then the body is functioning at its optimal potential.

So, what is a truth that has been shared for all time? Well, when I started to seek deeper and wanted to learn more about who we truly are, I started to look for a common theme that was shared in all religions. I started to study Buddhism, Hinduism, Taoism, Zen Buddhism, I Ching and so many others. I wanted to see if there was a common thread, a common message.

What I found was more than just that. It opened up my doors to a whole different understanding of the world than I have ever experienced before. I started to realize how true life is such a game. It exposed me to Universal Laws and the understanding of quantum physics started to put things together. As I started to enter Chiropractic school, I wanted to learn more and dive deeper than just learning about the nervous system. I started to study what Reiki was, Reconnective Healing, Two-Point Touch Therapy, Matrix Energetix and many others. I started to understand the fabric of what our bodies were, but more importantly, who we really were.

Through these experiences, it had showed me a path, a vision, of the essence of who we are. It had me seek out to mediums and talk to family members, friends and others who have passed on. It started to open up a world to understand what we see in this world is similar in the world we will end up in, which is home.

I started to see how things were connected and started to realize who I truly was, and as I continued to dive deeper into rediscovering who I truly was, I started to realize more of who we truly are. I started to understand on a deeper level, who we all are and how we are all part of something that is beyond anything I could write in words.

From this deep understanding, I started to see who I truly was and this opened up the door to more experiences than I could ever imagine. I have always believed that you have to live your life, your experiences and your belief systems to be like an investment portfolio. The more diverse it is, the better it is.

For me, the more diverse I went out and studied different religions, beliefs, the mind and so much more, I started to grasp deeper understandings. I want you to think of it like the United States. Who represents the United States? Who makes up the United States? Is it the government? Is it our Constitution? Is it our Founding Fathers? No. It's you. It's me. We make up the United States. It is the people who live, share time, experiences and memories here in the United States that makes up the country. From there, that gives power to the Government. That gives power to the Corporations. Without the people of the United States, the government could neither exist nor have its power. The Corporations could not have its power. It only does because of the people who live in the United States that makes up the country.

Another way to think of it is the difference of culture when you visit Chicago vs Los Angeles vs Austin. The people, the way of living, and the culture is what makes up that city. It is what gives it a vibe, an experience. But would you agree that each way of living, culture and vibe of each of those cities are different from one another?
So, the question is asked again, "Who are you?" Who are we, really? Well, it is quite simple. I am not going to share some elaborate response. Who you truly are is an eternal, infinite being. As Wayne Dyer has said, "We are a spiritual being having a human being experience." Where you are right now, reading this, is not your home. You are visiting this beautiful place called,

"Earth" and having a human being experience in it. It is as simple as that. But I want you to see the depth of how amazing being alive at this time is.

You are experiencing what it is to be human. To understand the human experience and to grow and expand through this experience. Think of Earth as a big spiritual University. The curriculum of this school is all the relationships, people, loved ones, family, friends, etc., that you interact with throughout your time on this planet. We are all here to help one another learn, grow and evolve. And, where you were born, grew up, was raised, etc., all play a role in your experience.

For example, why was I born and raised in Melrose Park, IL? Why did I have the parents I had? Why did I choose the friends I had chosen or grew up with? Why did I end up becoming a Chiropractor? Why did I not play baseball for the Chicago Cubs? How did everything lead up to having my wife? Why (eventually as I do not have kids during this time of writing) did I end up with having the kids that I have?

Everything in life happens for a reason. And this reason is simple. Rediscover who you truly are, expand in the areas of your life and evolve to who you desire to be.

You, the true YOU, is timeless and spaceless. You exist beyond time and space. As God is timeless and spaceless and has existed before time and will continue to exist after time, so shall you.

So, does that make you God? Well, from the Bible, it states we are made in the like-image of God? So my question to you is this…

If you are made from cotton threads to make your shirt, are you cotton? Or are you something else? If you are water that exists in a small cup but comes from an infinite source of water, are you part of that water or entirely different?

The one question I never had answered in the beginning of my journey was, if we were made in the like-image of God, how can we not be God? How can we not have similar power like God? When I asked these questions, I would have a huge emotional response and all I wanted to understand is, how can you be made part of something but not be part of that?

"You are not a drop of the ocean but the entire ocean within a drop."

Rumi

This sums up your Truth of who you are. You are God and God is all of us. I want you to think of it as a hologram. Remember back in the 80s and 90s they had those holograms with people's faces printed on there and many other images. They were kind of cool looking as they were 3D in a glass. This kind of breaks down how you are God and God is you.

If you took that hologram and broke it up into 1 million pieces, the image that was in there when it was whole, is still there in whole. It is just in a smaller piece. If you took a microscope and no matter how small the piece is, you would see the face in its full entirety in there. Pretty cool?

I thought so when I discovered this, but my other discovery of this was within the body. This is what made the most sense to me and it was through Chiropractic school to where I truly started to truly understand God. You have 38-75 trillion cells that make up your physical body. Within all those cells contains all the DNA to make up the body. For example, your eye cells have all the DNA to produce your entire body just as much as your skin cells, liver cells, nerve cells, stomach cells, muscle cells, heart cells, etc. do. All of the wisdom and knowledge needed to create you is within one single cell. But, those cells show up different with different sizes, functions and so forth due to what DNA is turned on and what DNA is turned off.

You make up one cell that makes up the body of God. Every other single soul that exists makes up other parts of the body of God. We all contain the same stuff, same potential, immortality and so forth. Each of us has a unique and special talent that no other soul has. It is the true reason how the body of God could ever exist. If there were two, there would be no need for one. God created you out of need rather than desire.

Why is that? Why would an omnipresent "spirit" need another soul? Isn't God all knowing? Isn't God all powerful? Isn't God the creator of all things? Everything that is in existence is from God. And yet, all of Creation is God.

But the question I had for myself that I would figure out later in life was that, when you are all knowing, and know every single thing that exists, how exciting is that? Imagine your life. Imagine that you knew every step of the way how things were going to turn out. You knew every single thought, emotion and how things were going to play out. How exciting would your existence be? How much would you truly learn about yourself and other experiences?

This is the need rather than the desire of why we were created. God created us all within an instant. And within that instant, we were given the greatest gift of all, "FREE WILL." God stated, go out, experience and enjoy all the infinite vastness and experience all that is there to experience in this Universe and the infinite other universes. That is right, there is infinite other universes than just our own.

From this, God would learn about itself through us and as it desires to exist to learn, grow and expand, the desire for us is the same. So from this, our main role is to create, grow, expand into the infinite vastness of your own universe. And through your own universe, God grows, expands and evolves just as you do and every other soul that exists does. God basically created every soul to learn about itself and continue to learn about itself.

One way to think about this is through our own children that we have. We learn about our children and watch their lives be created right in front of us. Even though we are wiser (sometimes) and have more experiences, we allow for the most part, our children to experience life on their own with our support. God works in the exact same way. God wants you to experience your soul's existence on its own and support you along the journey. God knows the exact thing to say, be, and help you feel because God is YOU. All things are extensions of God. So God lives through you and through you, it experiences and learns more about itself.

Now, this was not a thought I just came up with in life. This was 10-15 years of reading books, watching documentaries, endless hours of mediations, deep insights, talking with Shamans, studying Native Americans, different Tribes beliefs, Yogis, Buddhist Monks, different religions groups, Near Death Experiences (10,000 plus cases), mediums, different spiritual rituals, and family members who have passed over to the other side of the veil and more. From all of this, and my own experiences, I have been able to understand at a deep, profound level of who we are and I know this is just the beginning.

The best part of life is that YOU ARE LIFE. Your soul gives life to this body. It is what gives it an opportunity to function and exist. And it is a union ship with self to enjoy this body for the time you have to have an experience called, "Human being." When you break down the world Human, Hu = God in Sanskrit and Man = Physical. So when you put human together, it means God in physical form.

When we understand our language and our words, you will start to realize how it creates our reality. We will talk more about this in chapters to come.

I hope this is making sense and that if you are reading this, you didn't stop after we talked about the God part. I have met so much resistance when it comes to talking about how YOU are God and God is YOU. But I wanted to put this in the book so you can understand the Creator that is within you and what creates life and all of your experiences. I wanted you to feel and understand that regardless of what happens, the Universe is working FOR you not AGAINST you. The world can never be AGAINST you. The world responds to what YOU put out there. What you desire and focus on.

So who we truly are, are the Creators on the front line of physical reality. We are paving the way of existence and experiences. We choose based on our decisions and what we focus on and are leading the way. You chose to come here, in this lifetime, in this body, with your parents, siblings, friends, town, etc., to gain experiences and be one of the leaders in paving the way of physical reality. How powerful is that? Everything you experience in your life, helps pave the way for others but more importantly for God. All the things we do, we benefit but so does God. It is the best win-win you could ever dream of.

This is why when someone says, "God bless you," you are already blessed by God. God blessed you the moment you were created and always will be a part of your life as God lives through you throughout eternity.

God wants you to experience all the possible experiences that exist in this Universe and the infinite other universes. For that, when you grow, expand and evolve, so does God. For when you experience both sides or the shades of grey of life, so does God. We are on the front line of experiencing and creating physical reality and the beautiful part of it, not only does God benefit, grow, expand and evolve, all that we do, allows for other souls to do the same.

It is the most interdependent system I have ever witnessed or seen. This is where I came up with the quote:

"We are the bloodline for God and God is the bloodline for us."

God would never terminate Itself because why would It be unwilling to exist? This is why we will always exist in some form. How cool is that?

This information alone, should shed the fears of death. This should add light to the fear of death that you never die. You will NEVER die. There are cultures in this world that celebrate death, not mourn over it. They understand that you continue on in a new form, in a new life. Death is a disguise for a new birth. The moment your soul entered the physical body, it was a death in some form but a birth on another. The same is true for your physical life. The physical life will cease to continue to exist, but your soul will continue on. It never ends.

And based upon all the things I have researched and experienced, to end another fear of life was something that was embarked on by me at such an early age. "If I was not a good boy growing up and live a good life with all these rules to follow, I would not be worthy of heaven and would end up living in hell forever." How the heck would God, abandon his children and put them in eternal hell? Why the hell would God want to make his own children suffer? Why would a parent truly want, deep down, to have their child suffer temporarily and even further, for eternity.

To me, it never made sense, and when I challenged it, people would get upset, or even say, I would rot in hell when all I wanted to do was challenge an idea to see where the truth was in all of it.

Truth be told, there is no hell. Hell is only a place that exists within the mind that you created just as much as there is no fear, except the fear you create within your mind. These two constructs are just something created within your mind. Now for some people, they may read this and say, well, we have original sin and we were born from imperfection.

My challenge has always been, what does sin mean? How can I be born into this world and have a sin that no matter what I do in my entire existence in this physical life, I would never be able to get rid of it? It never made sense to me. And as I did my research, meditations and experiences, I started to see what truly sin was.

Sin comes from archery. When you sin in archery, it means you miss the mark. When you look at the sins you commit in your life, it is not what the religious world wants you to believe to where you can only confess to a priest or pray to Jesus to be forgiven. Truth be told, sin means being away from your purpose. Being away from what you desire to achieve.

Growing up in an Italian Roman Catholic household, I had so much sin; I thought I would never be good enough. I thought I was never worth much because every single day, based upon my upbringing, I had so much sin, a whole lifetime couldn't clear that shit out. But instead, it was the programming in my head I had to clear out, and from there, my journey into believing in myself started to change. And then, I wanted to understand what words came from and meant because from there, I would have a deeper understanding of their meaning.

So, sin is just missing the mark of your purpose. Here is what is amazing about this. Your purpose is decided for you by you. You are the one who chooses your purpose and your destiny. The moment you create a sin, is when you are being distracted in life and not being focused on what you want to achieve, desire or attract. It is as simple as this.

How powerful is that? Do you feel the power? Do you feel how it is YOU who has the choice?

Many people who were either at a near death experience which means, they died, but they came back to life eventually and they shared their experiences from the moment between. Over 10,000 cases have been documented and I will tell you, all of them say similar things. They are different in their own ways, and for the sake of the book, I won't dive into that but, they share one common theme. At the end, they realized that, everything came from them. Everything they experienced, chose and had in their life was from them and them only. All things worked FOR THEM and not against them.

Knowing this information and knowing that you always have a choice, can you see how it takes away this mind virus of we are not in control of our lives and instead, the truth serum states, we are in full control because at the end of the day, we were given a gift from God as being creators and that was, FREE WILL.

When we realize we always have FREE WILL, anything you choose to have, experience, BE, etc., is all up to you. And this process is never ending for that the word, "process," means a continuum of events, series and things. It means a never-ending. And you, my friend, are a process that never ends.

I want you to understand that when it comes to your process, imagine all the things you have learned in this life. Imagine 100 years of studying 3 main things. How well would you know them? How much of a master would you be? How many things would you not know? How much could you dive deeper into what you already know?

There is so much information and experiences to obtain, the process is infinite because there is always new experiences and paths being created. There are always new worlds and universes being created for us to experience so we can grow, evolve and expand to knowing and learning more of who we are just as God does through us.

The most amazing gift we were ever given is life. Life as a spiritual being. God created us through His breath of life and from there, we existed. Since our existence, God told us to go out, play, have fun and enjoy the infinite playground that will exist. There is so much for us to experience that 1 million lifetimes cannot fulfill. And isn't it great that we do last forever? That we may evolve, change and expand but the main fabric of who we are, is eternal?

At this point in this chapter, you start to realize, I hope, that you are not a title. I am not a chiropractor. I am not a son. I am not a husband. I am not an uncle. What I am is eternal, everlasting, spirit made from LOVE from God. What I am in this lifetime is still the same, but what I am doing is experiencing life as a chiropractor in my own way. I am experiencing what it is to be a son in my own way. I am experiencing what it is to be a husband in my own way. I am experiencing X, Y, Z in my own way just as you are.

At the end of all of this, it is just an experience. Something for us to grow, evolve and expand. It is the playground for rapid growth. Earth is a massive playground for us to just have fun, enjoy the process and experience all that you can in this world. It truly is meant for that. And my hope in this entire book is to lay out a guide to help you live an inspired and fulfilled life, regardless of what earth year you are at (age).

Before we come to the end of this chapter, I want to leave you with one more thought. It is a universal law shared by a man named, "Darryl Anka." Darryl Anka is a medium who channels information from an entity named, "Bashar." You can learn more about

Bashar's work by visiting, www.Bashar.org. Now for some of you, this may frighten you or say this is woo-woo stuff but understand that I never just jump in without analyzing. In this life, I was gifted with a very strong left brain (analytical). I have read and listened to Bashar share about life and all of what we do and who we are. Long story short, I have meditated on these concepts and looked at what other cultures shared about these concepts and the beauty is, I haven't found them to be wrong or inaccurate. Take this with a grain of salt, but I invite you to think, just for a moment, how if these are true, what does this mean for you?

There are 5 laws of creation based upon Bashar. These 5 laws are the Basics of Universal Laws. And as a law, it has been tested over and over to be true. I took the scientific method to these 5 laws and I can totally relate these to be true and will share my experiences with you.

1st law of creation states - You Exist.

This one is obvious. You exist or else you would neither be experiencing this book, nor your life. You exist and have always existed before time and will continue to exist after time. As the Law of Thermodynamics states:

"Energy is never destroyed or created, it just changes form."

Since you are made up of energy, you will always exist. The soul of who you are is an extension of God that will live for eternity. Awesome sauce, right? :)

Remember I stated before, you will always exist in some shape or form. Let science tell you how that works. Law of Thermodynamics is something I have been so happy to discover and apply to different aspects of life. What I have learned in the process is that, when you die, your energy is not destroyed nor do you not exist. What ends up happening is, your energy changes form into a new existence.

I want you to think of this as water. Let us say your physical form right now, is a cup of water. In that cup, you take on the vessel (cup) and fulfill its shape. During your time, you get to have an experience of what it is like to be a cup. When you choose your time is done to be a cup, your cup of water will be poured into another shape or form, let's say a water bottle. And now, you experience that water bottle and what those experiences are.

As you continue, this process lasts forever. And you never evaporate or have your water run out because Law of Thermodynamic states, "Energy is never created nor destroyed, it just changes form." This is why you will exist forever in some shape or form.

2nd Law of Creation states - Everything is Here and Now

This is a hard one for the human mind to comprehend. When we return back home in the spiritual form, we truly understand this and experience this. There is no time. Time does not exist. Everything is happening instantaneously. In our human mind, we think there is a past and a future. But really, it is all happening at the same time. Talk about mind explosion when you try to figure it out. The thing is though, our minds are not capable to handle this information at the higher level, it is saying that who you were at 1-year-old is now just as your older version exists. This occurs in the spiritual aspects simultaneously but within our physical reality, we see our child self in the past and who we are, within the now.

The thing behind this law is something called, "The Power of Now." Eckhart Tolle wrote a great book on this that discusses the power of now. All that you can ever experience is all in the present moment. It is in this exact moment you are reading this book.

You see, your past can only exist in the present just as much as your future can only exist in the present. When you are in the present moment, all that exists is what is in front of you. But once you start thinking of your past, you go into the past from the present moment just as much as you go into the future from the present moment. But you can never be in the present moment and the future at the same time. All that exists is the present moment.

3rd Law of Creation - The One is All and the All are One

This truly explains the interdependent relationship of how we are God and God is us. God is in every single existence. Nothing can exist without God. God penetrates all living things and all living things come from God. But at the same token, all living things are made from the same fabric as God.

This is why I used the analogy of the human body. This proved it to me as I saw the 38-75 trillion cells that exist within the body and how they all work together for the existence of the human body. All the souls that exist give expansion, growth and evolvement to and for God. And God supports us in the process for our own growth, expansion and evolvement.

4th Law of Creation - What you put out is what you get back.

Everything in this Universe works under another Law we will discuss later called, "The Law of Attraction." The law of attraction states like attracts like. It is what you put out into the Universe that you will get back in return. Universe = God. God will only give you what you ask for. God wants you to experience your soul's burning desire and physical desires. As long as you ask, focus, and stay consistent with it, God will arrange the rest to make that happen for you. At the end, it is for the experiences you choose to experience what you experience, God does also.

5th Law of Creation - Everything changes, except the first four laws.

Change is inevitable. Think about your life and how much has changed in your own life and the life of others that you have witnessed? Your body is in a constant change. Three to five days ago, you had a different intestinal lining than you do now. A month ago, you had different skin cells than you do now. 120 days ago, you had different blood cells than you do now.

Your body is constantly changing and never staying the same. Even your nerve cells change and replace themselves every 7 years. The beauty is, you see this in nature and the Universe also. Nature is always changing, adapting and improving just like your human body. The universe does the exact same thing. The physical universe has stars be created and destroyed. It has planets be created and destroyed. On a bigger level, there are universes that are created and destroyed.

We are always in a constant flux of change, even our souls for our soul, is in a process that is forever changing, expanding and evolving into eternity.

When we decide to plan out our life, create the blueprint, work with other souls, spirit guides, guardian angels and so forth to help us achieve what it is we desire to experience in this life, it allows for us to have rapid growth, expansion and evolvement. This is why Earth is known as a, "Spiritual University." It is a place where souls can come and gain rapid growth and expansion. It is for us to learn something but then, put it to the test. How cool is that?

For example, as ErikChanneling.com states:

"You can learn how to make brownies in the spiritual world, but in order to truly learn them, you have to go to Earth to gain that experience."

Being a human being is a great way to do the work on what you want to learn while being in spirit, you come up with the ideas.

Life is all about what you want to experience and you have the Universe supporting every choice you make.

Now, in the chapters to come, I will share with you other laws and methods to help you learn about the Game of Life and how to truly manifest all that you choose to experience.

Like every game, there are rules to it, and in this universe, there are specific laws that work in it. But in another Universe, these would not work. Imagine trying to play baseball with basketball rules. How well would that work out? How much chaos would happen?

So, I want to thank you for taking time to read this book and to invest into rediscovering the greatness you already are.

So let us begin…

Chapter 2

Focusing On Source Energy

"Always remember, your focus determines your reality"
George Lucas

What you focus on is what allows for your source energy to manifest and create into your reality. It is this focus that gives life to all that you experience and it all comes from you. You are the one who chooses what to focus on. You are the one who chooses what to experience and desire in your life. It all starts with you and only you.

In chapter one, we explained what this source energy is all about. It is the true essence of who you are and where all things come from. Everything that you have experienced in your life is from your own creation. Everything! Not one thing by accident.

Many people believe that things happen to them. The mindset of being a victim continues to grow. I have heard it so many times in so many ways. Hell, to be transparent, even I have fallen under the thought of being a victim. It is so ingrained in our heads but truth be told, that is an illusion. You can never be a victim of anything if you chose it. If you created it.

When you focus on something, you tap into your creative power. It is the power of your source energy that gives life to all things. One has to remember that you are life and within you is what gives life to this body. It is the intelligence that runs this body. It is what takes water and makes it part of your body. It is this intelligence that takes the last meal you ate and turns it into part of your body. There is no technology that exists in this world to make that happen so precious and perfect every single time.

So, your focus is this power and when you focus in on things, it is then, you give power to something. I want you think of this power like a toaster. If you never plug into the source, the energy that gives life to the toaster, how well will the toaster work? Same thing goes for a blow-dryer, refrigerator or anything that needs a source of energy to function. You are that source energy that gives life to all things and allows for it to exist and manifest into your realty. You are that source.

When I first started my chiropractic business, I studied all the leaders in our profession to understand in depth, how to be successful and how to run a very high profitable business while at the same time, being the best chiropractor I could be for my patients. I kept seeking answers to vague things concerning my profession. I kept looking at different seminars to attend and different mindset workshops to help me get into that state of manifesting what I desired.

I studied all the top marketing tools to achieve in social media. I studied all the philosophical, science and art. I would spend 2-4 hours a week studying the science, literature and research to make sure I was on top of my game. I studied all the different type of nutritional programs, diets, the best exercises to perform and so much more. It was a crazy process and something that was tiresome. No wonder I was burnt out and had a sense of being overwhelmed most of the time.

Even though, I learned a ton and it helped me become a better chiropractor, the goals and dreams of what I desired were not happening. I kept finding more and more lack happening in my business and in my life. I was not feeling the sense of abundance and felt more of a sense of scarcity.

What I started to realize was, I had the best computer system in the world, but I was never plugging it in. I started to realize, I was trying all the magical ways to push the buttons, turn it on, put new graphics cards in, new processors and all that wonderful stuff BUT never took the time to plug it in.

Then, when I finally started to plug into the source of who I am, the source that gives life to my body, was the moment I started to feel something different. Things started to run smoother. Things started to get easier. I didn't have to have the answers to all things as if I trusted the process, it would all work out for the best in the end. And the more I focused on me, the source of all things, is when I started to see my life shift. It was then, I started to actually feel complete.

Now, to be truthful, this did not happen instantaneously. Anyone that tells you, I made a decision and boom, it was done, is lying to you. And I am not only speaking from experience, but even the way the mind works, you have to recondition your mind. You have to retrain how your brain was working and put in a new software program to have it run off. This takes some time and some conditioning but it will happen.

I started to realize that I was doing things backwards. I was focusing on what I wanted to HAVE first and then focused on what I needed to DO in order to BE the person I wanted to become. This is a flawed model that focuses on the lack. This focuses on the things that you are not. The things that you do not have.

You see, since everything in your reality is determined by what you focus on, what you give life to, if you focus on lack, what will you experience more of? If you focus on what you don't have, what will you experience more of? The lack. The things you don't have.

Just like my story, I thought I didn't have all the answers and I needed to research and study as much as possible to achieve these answers to obtain the success I desired. To become the leader in my community when it comes to living your maximized human potential. But in all reality, what I was focusing on was, I wasn't enough. I needed to have all this extra knowledge and information in order to make myself feel good until someone with more knowledge and information came along. Not a great recipe for success.

Instead, when I started to focus on me being good enough. When I started to focus on myself being the doctor I chose to be which was the leader in helping individuals maximize their human potential, things started to shift and change. It was then, I started to see a difference in my business, in the patients we were attracting in the office and much more. I was going to the source and focusing on who I had to BE rather than what I needed to HAVE first.

Once I started focusing on who I had to BE, it was then everything shifted. For now, I was tapping into my source, my intelligence rather than looking outside of it.

From there, I started to look around and say to myself, "Who do I want to BE?" Why do I want to BE that person? What will it give me? What will I feel if that happens and why is this so important to my heart? I started to seek into deep questions and take time to answer them. I wouldn't just answer them from a mental state but more of a heartfelt state. I would focus inward and see what would show up for me.

From this experience, I started to realize my anxiety started to calm down. I was not as anxious as I used to be. Because, in order to achieve what I chose to experience in my reality (life), I realized I just needed to focus on me and who I needed to BE.

You see, your focus dictates your reality in a very simple process.

Where your focus goes, energy flows. Where energy flows, manifestation grows. Where manifestation grows, becomes your reality (your life/ your experience).

This is a universal principle of our Universe on how it works. Both in the physical realms and the spiritual realms. It is all about how we focus and what we focus on. Since you are made up of energy, wherever your focuses go towards gives life to that. Energy is what gives life to the entire universe, this planet and yourself. Energy is what makes all of this possible. Within your human body is a shell, a coat that contains the energy within it.

When you truly grasp and understand this principle, you will become more aware and conscious of what you focus on because you know this is happening all the time rather you believe it or not.

Let us use the BE, DO, HAVE model to explain how someone would become a millionaire. It is something many people strive for or desire to have. When it comes to how you will attract a million dollars, many people think of winning the lotto, working endless hours, etc. The reasons are infinite, but the point is, we believe once we have this money, we can do the things we love and be the person we want to become.

But, let's reverse this and go along the BE, DO, HAVE model. Now, ask the question, who do I have to BE in order to become a millionaire? Where does this take your focus to? Who are you focusing on?

It shifts the focus from outside of you to within you. And now, you start to look at the ways you have to BE on a physical, mental and emotional level. This concept will help you achieve all that you desire in this lifetime.

I remember reading a quote and it stated, "Instead of focusing on making that million dollars, how about focusing on who you have to BE and the journey of the transformation to become that millionaire instead."

I love this quote because once again, it focuses on you and what you have to transform to become. What is it that you have to BE and shift your energy to manifest all that you desire? Remember, like attracts like, and in order to attract what it is you choose to experience, you have to raise your vibration/energy to that level in order to make that happen. We will be discussing this in chapters to come.

So going back to my story of who I had to BE, I shifted my focus to creating a practice that saw a lot of pediatrics, pre-natal and fertility. It took some time because when I made that decision, my office only saw about 5-10% of this group. But I knew what it meant to me and how I knew I wanted to help children lead on the path they were designed to be, living their maximized human potential every single day of their lives. And based upon my upbringing and all the health challenges I had faced, to even coming close to death around the age of 5, I didn't want to see another kid go through what I had to go through. And if I am able to help a child live to their potential without any of that, I have succeeded and I will feel fulfilled.

Understanding this concept, is the BEING aspect. So, again, the question is who did I have to BE? I had to be a voice for children and educate parents on the health of children. I started to create videos on why it was important to have a child's nervous system checked for subluxations (misalignments in the spine that cause miscommunication between the brain and the body). I made it my mission and used myself as an anchor to always keep me focused on what I wanted to create.

You see, there is something magical about looking in a child's eyes. I have heard from pediatric seminars that, when you look at a child's eyes, it helps the adult heal the inner child within them. I don't know how true this is, but I can only speak from experience. And every time I see a child smile as I look deep into their eyes, it is like me looking to my inner child's eyes and letting him know, it is all going to be OK.

From there, as I continued to focus on me and choosing to BE, my life transformed within a year. Our office went from seeing 5-10% of pediatric patients to 40-50% within the first year. And, I felt more fulfilled every single day. It was something I was seeking but didn't realize it was always in me. I was not focusing on me and instead giving my power away until one day, I turned it back within and focused there. After that, everything shifted and changed and now, I have the practice I always dreamed of. And at times, it even looks like a day care center and I couldn't be happier because deep down, I know I am helping these kids live their maximized human potential, every single day of their lives. Imagine what will happen for them in 5 years? 10 years? 20 year? The infinite potential is unreal and unfathomable.

So, what is it that you are focusing on? What is it that you want to achieve? What is it that you desire to experience? Remember, where you are in your life right now is as a result of all the things you focused on that created these things into your reality.

Take a moment to look at the things that are happening in your life. Look at the things you are happy about. Think about the things you are not happy about. Focus on how much power you give to these things. Because you will only experience more of what you focus on.

Let us share another story. This is a Cherokee Legend. An old Cherokee is teaching his grandson about life. "A fight is going on inside of me," he said to the boy. "It is a terrible fight and it is between two wolves. One is evil - he is anger, envy, sorrow, regret, greed, arrogance, self-pity, guilt, resentment, inferiority, lies, false pride, superiority, and ego." He continued, "The other is good - he is joy, peace, love, hope, serenity, humility, kindness, benevolence, empathy, generosity, truth, compassion, and faith. The same fight is going on inside you and inside every other person, too."

The grandson thought about it for a minute and then asked his grandfather, "which wolf will win?"

The old Cherokee simply replied, "The one you feed."

No matter what happens in your life, what you will experience is all based upon the wolf that you feed. It is all based upon what you focus on. In this story, when the grandfather stated, "the one you feed," is the life energy, life force, source energy that exists within you that feeds into the reality of what you experience. You are the one who continues to give life to your experiences and only you can change your experiences. No one else can.

You see, you are the producer, the actor, the screen writer, the writer, the cast, the main actor, and the other actors of your life. You are the one who writes the script and how the movie will play out. It is you and only you. No one else can change the script or change the movie except you.

I will share another story with you about this concept.

There was a lady who was home alone. When she was home alone, in the evening, she heard something downstairs and went down to see what it was. As she started to go downstairs, she saw a man in an all-black outfit walking around her house. She panicked and ran upstairs. The man heard her running up the stairs and started to follow her. As she ran back into her bedroom to hopefully protect herself from this man, he broke the door down and entered.

As she was freaking out for her dear life, she screamed at him, "What do you want from me? What will you do to me?" The man replied, "Lady, this is your dream. You are the one calling the shots here."

Did that get your heart racing? I know it did for me, but once again, this is the dream we live called, "Life." In this life, all the things that happen to us are from us. The universe is always working FOR us, not AGAINST us.

You are the source of what creates your life and gives to your life. It is what gives life to all your experiences and you are the one who change it in the beat of a dime.

Now, you may read this and say, "This may be too simple." The truth is, this is the easiest part. Just focus on what you desire and it will manifest into your reality. But, in our modern day, we have made it harder and harder to stay focused. The problem with our society today is, we have way too many distractions that pull us away from what it is we desire.

Whether it be your children, your job, social media, the mainstream media (news), etc., there is something that is always trying to take you away from what you want to focus on. It can be circumstances in life. It can be anything. All these things are what pull you away from what you desire and in that process, when you become distracted, it muddies the water. It creates a subluxation to the message. And now, the Universe, that is working FOR you, doesn't know what you want. You are saying one thing one day, then changing it up the next day and never staying focused on what it truly is you desire.

Remember that in life, a confused mind will always say no. One of my former business coaches used to tell me that all the time. And I started to do this in different aspects of my life and started to notice when they were confused, they most of the time would say no. When it came to sharing information with practice members and informing them on what they have going on. When I started to notice they were confused, it was those that would most of the time, say no to wanting to work with us in the office.
Once I started to practice this principle and made things much simpler and straight forward, it was amazing on how my conversions in my office went through the roof. We would roughly hit around 85-100% each month. And it wasn't some script I was saying. It wasn't some new selling technique I was using. I was just being raw, real, simple and relevant to my practice members and that resonated with them.

As we carry on here, we have a beautiful life. Life is so amazing and the Universe will always let you know if you are on track with the things you envisioned to create. To show you, how much you are truly focusing on the things you chose to experience. Since we live in a time/space continuum, the things that we choose to experience do not happen instantaneously and for many, this is a blessing. Imagine that every thought you focused on would happen instantaneously, how insane would life be? All the worries that you have would happen instantaneously just as much as the joy you desire to experience. Thankfully, we have this time/space continuum to allow for the time and space to occur at a specific moment.

With this system, it allows for you to work on your focus and make sure to stay focused on the prize. Always stay focused on the end in mind. This is why I am a big component of focusing on your vision rather than your goals. Your vision is what you want to see happen and the steps to get there, you leave up to the Universe. You learn to trust the process and why wouldn't you want to?
The Universe works FOR you and if you have a system that works for you, it will always support you in every single choice you make. Talk about unconditional love. The Universe/God wants to expand, evolve and experience itself. It will experience itself in all

shades of color. It allows for you to choose what it is you want to experience and the Universe/God will experience the same thing. This is why we are on the front lines of creating in this physical reality. It is so cool and so amazing to be living in these times, and any time for that matter.

So with a time/space continuum, what that means for you is, after a specific amount of time and space, the Universe will provide for what it is that you desire. It shows up in an infinite amount of ways to guide and lead you there. So, when we look at a new focus and a new vision, the Universe will show you at a specific given time if you are on track. It will show you that you are on track or not. How cool is that? You have a built-in system to let you know, if you truly are focusing in the right direction or not.

Let me share a story with you. When I started to become more focused in my business about working with children and working with helping families and adults live to their maximized human potential, I would notice when I would not be focused. I would notice when I was distracted because, in one month, we would see a surge of new families and children and then the next month, we wouldn't see any. And I would tell myself, "What am I doing wrong? Why are we not keeping the momentum moving forward?" I would ask my staff what is happening and before you know it, I catch myself in a drift away from my vision. My focus had shifted. Then, I would catch myself, refocus and reinstate what my vision was and what I wanted to accomplish. From that moment, sometimes it happened in a week, 2 weeks or even a couple months, but things would shift and we'll be back on track with the vision.

This is an endless process that happens to us all. Even with patients in my office. Sometimes, life happens and gets in the way of their intention of working towards being their best version of them and I will say, "The key thing is to rebound back on track and make up for any lost time." The longer you stay away from your vision, the harder it will be to get back on track and even harder for you to attract it into your reality (life).

The other factor that muddies the water and disrupts your focus is your past conditioning. Your past conditioning is what you believe things are to be. These past conditionings come up from time to time but mostly will show their power when things hit the fan. It is when you are stressed out they will fully take in power.

Growing up, for me, I always felt I couldn't be good enough. I had a father who was a perfectionist and he demanded that from me. No matter what I did, he would always find a fault with that. How did this affect me in life? How did this disrupt my focus and create a big distraction?

Well, if I saw a patient not get well or achieve the results they wanted within a specific time or even worse, within their timeframe they thought it should happen, I would feel like I failed them. When I set goals for myself and I hold myself to a very high standard with very high expectations (my poor wife), when I would fall short, which felt like often, I would think I was a failure. I would think I wasn't good enough. When I started to get stuck into these programs that I grew up with that I CREATED TO BE TRUE, it was then, I started to say to myself, maybe I wasn't good enough to achieve or be what I desired to be.

And from there, all the focus and all the things I desired to achieve, boom, gone. Why is that? Because I confused the Universe and made it focus on something completely different than what I was attempting to achieve before, which was, "Be the community leader in maximizing human potential."

How many of you go through this? How many of you allow for your past conditioning and stories take over your life and control your destiny? The thing is, you have the power to break away from these once you change your focus.

In this story that I have played so many times in my life hitting the rewind and replay button, I started to shift my focus into the positive of it. I went all the way back to when my dad would pick out something wrong with anything I did and I started to ask, "What if he was just trying to help me break through a comfort zone or limit that I have created within?" What if he was just trying to help me always strive to be better and never get comfortable?

The beautiful thing is, whatever I frame to be true and focus on, it will be. And so I started to look at it as a way to constantly strive for greatness and never settle and get comfortable with anything I do. I started to look at life as a way of infinite expansion and growth and never stopping in anything I do. It made me get good at something and then, focus on ways on how to improve to great, then to mastery and then to continue going deeper with things.

I had a choice to either focus on a low self-worth as an individual who is not good enough or I can focus on how this taught me that no matter how good I get at something, know that there is always a deeper and wider way of learning things. There is always something more I can learn. And this is the story I focus on which has become true for me.

You always have the power of choice and you create life to be whatever you want it to be. It is all about what you give your power to (focus/attention). I could have thought of myself as never being good at anything, and as long as I continued to focus on that, I would have seen it show up in my life. It would be the only reality I would ever experience unless I changed my focus. In a couple chapters from now, we will dive deeper into these concepts and talk much more in depth about stories, belief systems and what you focus on. So sit tight and continue reading. :)

So, how can your focus, what you give attention to, create your reality? How can this be so true?

You see, all the things that you experience within your physical world, the chair you sit on, the bed you sleep on, the cup you drink out of, the house/apartment you live in, the car you drive, the train you take, etc., has all come from a non-physical element first. All non-physical elements are what create the physical world. Everything has all resonated from a thought, from the mind first. You see, the law is very simple. Your mind tells your eyes what to look for.

When you focus on something, this will start within your mind. When you become focused on what it is you want to choose to experience, the eyes will now look for just that. So, when you focus on something and do not become distracted, it makes it so much easier for the eyes to know exactly what to look for.

Let us play a game. Take a moment and look at the FedEx logo. What I want you to find within that logo is the arrow and the spoon. This will determine how fast you can focus on an image once you have it within your mind.

How long did it take for you to find the spoon and the arrow? Did you notice the arrow points towards the X and the spoon is within the lower case E?

Why did I share this with you? Well, this is an example of how well you can focus. Once you see this, I promise you, every time you look at a FedEx logo or see a truck passing by, you will always look for the arrow and spoon now. Why will you notice this all the time? It's simple. Because your mind told your eyes what to look for. You have become aware of this now and may have never been before.

Let us use another example. Let's say you are going to buy/lease a new car. As you do your research and test drive, you finally have come down to a decision of which car you want. Once you buy/lease the car, as you are driving home or driving for the next week, you start to notice how many times you see your car on the road. You start to notice it more and more and more. Why is that? Why does this happen?
As from this chapter, it is very simple. Your mind tells the eyes what to see, and once you can focus on what to look for within the mind, it is easy to see within your physical experience.

As I am writing this book, my wife just leased a new car and she is not too big into cars, models and whatnot, but what has been funny is, she points out her car all the time on the road now. Amazing how this happens, but some may say you have created awareness of it which I agree but I like to say, you are easily able to focus on what it looks like and what to look for just like the FedEx logo. Watch how many times you look for the arrow and spoon when you look at the logo from now on. It gets me every time.

So, when you look at the things you desire to accomplish, achieve, experience, and so forth, always know, the power comes from you. You are the source energy and anytime you allow a distraction to take place, you are disconnecting from source just like you unplug the toaster while it is toasting your bread. You may have toasted the bread partially, but you did not fully toast the bread to where you wanted it to be.

As the law of creation states, "Everything you put out, echoes back at you." When you are hyper-focused on achieving your desire, you will send that off to the universe and the universe, when it has a crystal clear image, will send what you desire back to you as you have wished. The more you send a signal out to the Universe and are crystal clear upon it, the increased likelihood you will experience this in your reality.

Distractions show up in so many different forms, and one of the biggest reasons, if not, the #1 reason why people don't achieve what it is they desire in life is because they are not consistent with it. If you are not practicing consistency with what you choose to experience, you will never see it in your lifetime or it will take a lot of work and time to reap the benefits. Most of the time, when it comes to the choices we make, it is what creates our reality.

Your habits become your reality and what you do on a daily basis will either lead towards your desired experienced or something far from your vision. This is truly called, "Karma." Karma means action in Sanskrit. And unfortunately, the meaning of Karma has gone more towards what you do, will come back to you. So if you do good things, good things will come to you and if you do bad things, bad things will come to you. I cannot emphasize how much that is not true. I have tested this theory out in so many ways and what I have realized is the following. Karma is not a punishment factor but what Karma truly means, is the accumulation of your choices/actions you have taken to where you are now.

Karma is where you are right now. If you are feeling depressed and sad, this is the accumulation of choices you have made to allow for you to experience this state of emotions. You had to focus on the things that you are not achieving with consistency to create that experience in your life. Remember, all the things that you put out into the universe will come back to you. The accumulation of your focus each and every day will attract what it is you desire to experience. This is your Karma.

But, just because something is your Karma at this time doesn't mean you cannot change it. You are not chained down to your past choices and what you focused on. At any given time, you can start the creation of a new reality. You can, within an instant, tell the Universe, I am ready to experience something different and it will start getting to work for you. It will start looking at different circumstances, situations and people that you will need in order to achieve that experience. It is always working for you at any given time. Never forget that.

So, if you look at your Karma and you don't like where things are, change your focus to what it is you do desire. Focus on the things that you would enjoy and make you feel bliss. Those are the things, as long as you focus on them consistently, will create the experience you desire. It is impossible for it to not show up that way. You are the one who gives life to all creations. You give life to the creations of your own universe. It is what you pay attention to that gives life to. It is within its simplest form.

Let me share an example on how this works. Many people in America and parts of the world do not like our current president, Donald Trump. Regardless if you are for him or against him is up to you. This is not about being political, but I want to use what we have talked about and show you how this works. I want to show you how the mind tells the eyes what to see.

As I mentioned his name, you either felt good or bad about President Trump. Right off the bat, that is what you focus on. The second thing is, if I asked you, "Do you like Donald Trump as president?" Some will say yes and some will say no. I will then ask, "Why do you like or dislike Donald Trump?" And whatever you say next, is what you focus on. It is the things that you want to focus on the most, and most of the time, it will blur everything else out.

But this is only one example. Another example is when you first start dating someone. Everything seems to be magical. There appears to be nothing wrong with the person you are with. Some people call this, "The Honeymoon Phase." Why is it that you only find the good in the person and experience that in your reality? Why is it that you only see the positives of the person and the rest of who that person is, their negatives, are blurred away? Some may say, your mind neurologically is not functioning normally, and within a given time, it will start to see the negatives of the person.

For me, as you remember that your focus is what creates your reality and what you focus on, tells your eyes what to see. When you first start dating someone, you focus only on the good. You strictly focus on the good and don't allow for anything else to shine in. But then, over a period of time, you may have your first argument. You may have your first X, Y, Z that shows up and now, you start to focus on that. Your expectations of this person are starting to change and now you are not seeing things as you did before. You start to become aware of other things and you give life to them by focusing on them. As time goes on, you start to find more and more things that you dislike and give them power. Why now? Why are you seeing more of this? It is because you are choosing to focus on those things. You are giving it life. Those things were there before, but since you hyper-focused on the good, you didn't see the bad. And we all have positives and negatives within us. There is not one person in this world who is perfect. The only perfection is when two people come together. Their imperfections make up a couple of perfection.

And so, remember that this law of focus affects all aspects of your life. If you start to look only at the positives of your significant other, it is then, through training yourself to stay super focused on it, that will allow for you to see the truth of who they are and not let their other side get the best of you.

When I was in 9th grade, I remember I had an algebra teacher who was boring and someone I did not want to learn from. Since math and science were the two subjects I excelled in, I was receiving a C- in the class and I remember my mom asking me why I wasn't doing so well as I normally do. Of course, I blamed the teacher for this and said how boring he was and that I didn't like anything about him. And what my mom said next, changed my whole experience and grade for that matter. She said to me, "How about focus on the one thing that you like about him and if you can't find something, that means you are not looking in the right places." So for the next few weeks, in class, I would try to find one thing that I enjoyed about this teacher. It took me sometime but I will never forget it. I saw him help a troubled student who thought they wouldn't understand the concepts and wasn't doing well. He took his time, explained the problems, how to achieve the answers and showed that he cared. I said to myself, "He wants everyone to succeed and he is not out to get us." From that moment on, I started to focus on how he cared so much for his students and kept telling myself that story. I focused on it so hard, I would look for it until it showed up and it didn't show up every day, but I made sure, I didn't allow for any other distractions such as he is boring, etc., to chime in. Long story short, I kept up with that focus so much, my grade turned around from a C- to an A- within a couple months and finished the year off with an A- for the class.

Imagine if I kept stuck in the other reality believing of him to be a horrible teacher, boring, etc., what would have happened to my grade? Because my performance was only up to me and no one else. Nothing changed except me. And when I changed, my world changed in front of me.

What areas of your life are you focusing on the negatives more than the positives? What areas of your life do you not feel fulfilled and inspired with? Look at these areas and pay attention to what you focus on? Our mind is a couple million year old evolutionary program that is designed to focus on the negative and the things that are wrong. Just because our mind is designed to do that does not mean you don't have the power to change that. You don't have the power to view something different. You do.

The key to changing your life is changing your focus, and once you change your focus and consistently focus on what it is you give your power to, it is impossible to not manifest into your reality. Out of the entire chapter, this is the biggest concept I am trying to share with you. Consistency is the key to creating the life you desire. And with consistent action comes the chosen reality and no matter the circumstances you face, as long as you stay focused and stay consistent, nothing can stop you. This is where your true power lies because you are a creator and you are source energy. Don't let anyone else tell you something different.

As we have talked about focus, I wanted to tap into one more thing before we end this chapter and that is the stories and belief systems that you choose. The stories that you focus on is what becomes your reality. What story are you telling yourself daily? What story are you stating you are?

You see, my story about my dad always picking out something to be wrong in everything I do created two different stories, one that I am not good enough and one that, regardless of what I do, I can always become better. Which one is right? Some may say the first one. Some may say the second one. At the end of the day, what is right is the one I chose to believe in. It is the one I chose to focus on. The moment I chose to believe in that story, within a specific amount of time and space, it became my reality. And as long as I give life to that story, that belief system, it will continue to exist within my life until I focus/change the story.
Do you feel the power behind this? Are you starting to see how you create your life in whichever way you desire? The truth is, whatever story you tell yourself that you believe to be true, will be the experience you have in life. It doesn't happen any other way. So, I have something for you to do. I want you to look at yourself and see what stories you share with yourself that you believe in.

Look at the stories you talk about as being a significant partner to someone. Look at the stories you tell yourself about your career/business. Look at the stories you tell yourself about attracting the finances that you desire. Look at the stories you tell yourself about your physical health/body, mental state and much more. Look at these stories and start paying attention to what you are telling yourself. This is what you are focusing on and this is what is creating your reality.

When I was 12 years old, I had to wear the pant size called, "Husky." My mother just told me I am a big guy and this is the size I need to wear. I always felt overweight and never felt like I was in good shape compared to my dad and others. But at the age of 12, I asked my mom, "Can you teach me how to get a six-pack?" I focused, believed in the story that, a six-pack would bring me happiness and I am not talking about a six-pack of beer. :)

My mom taught me a few things, and as I started to focus more on not hating the way I looked but starting to envision my body molding into what I desired, the Universe started working for me. Within 3-4 months, my best friend lent me a non-weight lifting workout book for me to do. I worked out each week consistently. When I would look in the mirror, I wouldn't focus on what I didn't have, the lack, but instead, focused on the minor changes that showed me I was getting closer and closer to my goal. As I continued to focus on the positive changes that my body was making, my goal was coming to me faster and faster. And before you know it, it happened without me even noticing it. I know this sounds weird but I remember walking around the house shirtless and my mom noticed I achieved my goal and I was so focused on the positive changes of what I was doing and making sure I kept up with the work that I forgot about what the goal was. I got immersed into the journey of achieving the goal rather than making the goal my main outcome.

The key thing is, you have a blank slate of experiencing whatever experience you desire and you are the BOSS when it comes to it. You are the one who dictates what you desire and what will help you achieve your results. The Universe is always working FOR you. It is helping you achieve the experience you focus most on. And this is as easy as going on Netflix to watch a show. You pick the category of what it is you want to experience and then look for the show/movie that you want to experience.

It is the same concept as watching TV and looking at the 500-600 channels that exist and picking one that you are hyper-focused on. That is the one that will show up on your TV. The same is true for a radio station. If you want country music, in Chicago, the station is 99.5 FM. The tuner focuses strongly on the frequency of 99.5 FM and it gets country music for you. The same thing happens if you want current hits like B96 (96.3 FM in Chicago) or any other type of station. In order to achieve that station to experience that type of music, you have to focus in on the frequency in order to achieve it.

I know you may be saying, it can't be that easy but truthfully it is. You knew how this worked when you were a kid. You understood the simplicity of this. You never doubted it or judged it. It just happened for you and that is all you wanted to know. But eventually, we adults who don't know how this works anymore, start to teach the child how this doesn't work anymore and then, it starts to get lost as the child starts to shift his/her focus. And once focus shifts, everything else follows.

You can change the switch on what you see in others and in your life within nanoseconds. It all starts with you. Whatever you want to experience, whatever you want to make out of someone, it starts with you.

When I was in high school, I remember classmates would talk about a teacher and how they didn't like him/her. They would share all the reasons why and whatnot. I had an opportunity to either accept that story and belief system as real and start focusing on it which would turn into my experience or I could create a different story to believe in which would have shifted my focus elsewhere to create a different experience.

Since my experience with my math teacher all changed when I changed my focus upon him, I knew this to be true with all my other teachers. I started to see how, if I focus on what I want to focus on, it would change my experience. I have used this tool in many aspects of my life.

Focusing on what I want to see happen instead of what I believed before has changed all my relationships, especially my parents. I started to look back at how I was with my dad and how I viewed him. I started to see how I gave him no chance at all. I was so focused on how he wanted me to be perfect and I was never good enough, that it blurred all the good he was doing for me. It wasn't until my mid-twenties, when I started to see clearly now the rain has gone. :)

I started to change the story of what was and asked myself, "What if I rewrote the script and create a different story? What would happen then?" As I have shared with you, the relationship has drastically changed. Now, at my ripe age of 34 years better, I have an amazing relationship with my dad. It is one that I wished all my life but I knew, if I didn't change, it wouldn't have happened because it is my life, my reality, is all created from me and it is all based upon my focus. It doesn't happen any other way.

Guard your mind and be careful of what stories you believe in. Because the more you focus on the story, the more you give life to it to become your reality. And the cool thing about all of this is, if you don't like a story, create a new one…

You can change the story at any given time and it is as simple as changing the channel, picking a new movie on-demand, picking a station on Spotify or even choosing a radio station. Once you believe this to be that simple, it will be. It is whatever story you focus on. It is whatever wolf you feed. It is all up to you.

As we close in this chapter, remember this one quote that sums it all up.

> **"Whether you think you can, or think you can't, you are right."**
>
> *Henry Ford*

When it comes to your life, there is no right or wrong except what you believe for there to be. Only you decide and whatever you focus on, it shall be.

Chapter 3

Words Are The Fabric

"The magic of words is that they have power to do more than convey meaning; not only do they have the power to make things clear, they make things happen."

— Frederick Buechner

When we look at words, we look at them in the form of a way to communicate. We are using different words to express ourselves which in return, helps us communicate to another being what we are trying to convey. When we look at the way humans communicate and the different ways we do, there are over 7,000 languages in the world. (Source https://bit.ly/2dqD6QD).

We express ourselves in so many ways. It is amazing and this is just the use of language. 93% of communication is non-verbal. This means, we are looking beyond the words. What we find is that 55% of all communication is by the means of body language and the other 38% is determined by the tone that you use when communicating. So, words only make up 7% of communication with another human being. (Source: https://bit.ly/2wZTBuZ)

This also holds true for dogs. Dogs will pay more attention to your state of being (energy) and body language more than the words you use. Tone does work for dogs also. If you own a dog, try this out. Look at your dog and talk in a very happy tone of voice and say, "I love you." Watch how it wags its tale and responds in a positive way. Then, look at your dog and say in a mad voice, "I love you." What you will notice is a different response. I do this with my dog once and a while to just see how he responds. I would say words in a high tone happy voice and it would get excited. I would change my tone and say the exact same words and it wouldn't be as excited.

As we communicated fully in chapter two about focus, you will start to see how the words you focus on to utilize and communicate with others and how you communicate with yourself is the fabric to your reality. This is the building blocks to what you experience. It has been said, "Change the words you use and watch your world change." I have gone to many different seminars, studied many books on the power of language, words and how it creates the vibration to our reality. It is amazing how you change one word and it can play that much of an impact in your life. It has been told that, the average human being uses on a daily basis about 3,000 words. (Source: https://bit.ly/BuS6LI).

But what if I told you, if you expand the words you use, replace lower vibrational words with higher vibrational words, you truly will change your life and your experience. Why? How? Well, back to chapter 2, you are putting your attention upon a word to express something; that focus echoes out into the Universe, and what you put out into the Universe, will come back at you.

Remember that where attention goes, energy flows and wherever energy flows, manifestation grows. And when manifestation grows, your reality glows. I wanted to use "glows" to help rhyme with the rest. But what I meant by "glows" is, it becomes your reality. So, one of the laws is simple, "In order to change your life, you must change your words as they are the fabric to your reality." And when you allow for energy to flow, that energy comes from source energy just like electricity flows into something for you to use it.

Let us dive deeper into this concept to give you tools and ways to transform your life through the usage of words.

> **"Be sure to taste your words before you spit them out."**
>
> *Auliq Ice*

In other words, be conscious of the words you use. Just like we talked about in the last chapter about being conscious and aware of what you focus on, words are under the same surveillance.

Have you ever been told something and whatever that person has said, it stuck with you beyond that timeframe? For example, is there something that someone can say, choosing a word, that will trigger an emotional response? Sometimes, you can say something to someone and it may mold their thinking or play a huge influence in their life: positive or negative.

If you noticed in the book already, I do use the word, "desire," from time to time to connect with my audience, but you will see I heavily use the word, "choice" or "chose." Here is how words play a huge role in your life, and actually, this was an awakening for me just a few years ago.

I was reading a book on language and it talked about how when you say the word, "want" or "desire," you are focusing on the lack. You are focusing on something that you don't have. The more you focus on what you don't have, you end up experiencing more of the lack than what you desire. You cannot desire something without focusing on what you don't already have. You cannot want something if you don't have it already.

This was a turning point in my life as I stopped creating goals and started to work more on the vision. It was because of this reason right here. The more you focus on the vision, the more you let go of the control of what you want. And so, when I did my planning for the vision of what I wanted to achieve in my office and all the different visions that were created, I strongly focused on using words as I choose this experience to be the family wellness leader of my community. I choose because if you come from the same fabric as God, you lack nothing. You are complete and whole already.

Just like you pick a movie or show on Netflix, you don't have to do much work except just look, see, focus and click play. Not much work behind that. The same goes for who you are. You already have all the connections and resources needed to experience anything you choose. All you need to do is shift your focus to what you choose to experience and then, declare to the Universe, I choose to experience X, Y, Z and so it is done. This is a declaration to the Universe in crystal clear form of what it is you want to experience. You took the remote, pointed at the Universe and you stated, "I choose to experience X and so it is done." And the Universe will go to work to help you experience that experience you have chosen.

I have noticed over the years, vision boards have become more and more popular. I have friends who have many different ones and focus on the vision board for what they want. I used to own 7 different vision boards for 7 different aspects of my life and I would update them once per year. Sometimes, things worked out, half the time it didn't. I never understood why and maybe I wanted things more than others or maybe I was desiring and wanting rather than choosing.

In my experience, I have done vision boards since I was 24. I have done over 20 vision boards since that time. I would update my vision boards each year to what I desired and tried to get as specific as possible. I would sit there, visualize, and focus on what it is I desired. I just kept focusing my energy into what I wanted to experience with what I was looking at. I would spend 5-10 mins a day on this. But, 50-70% of the time, I wouldn't achieve what I desired. Until I realized, the words I was using were want and desire.

What do you think happened when I changed the words around, and stated, "I choose to experience X, Y, Z?" Things started to shift for me very quickly. I started to see things change in my life. From my marriage, to my business, to my mental health, physical health and so much more. I stepped into a place of power when I said, "I choose." And when I give my power back to me, source energy, and infinite potential is possible. There is no limit to what you choose to experience. None whatsoever.

I want you to look around you and see how all things that exist are expressing life. All things contain life. You are sitting there with your human body and within it, contains all life and intelligence within the physical limits of the human body. The same goes for me, a dog, cat, lion, elephant, etc. Life is all around us and we are just a bubble of that life. Within the bubble contains life which is in all bubbles that exist. But, the exterior of the bubble is completely different compared to any other bubble. We are vastly different on the surface but yet, within the depth of our bubble, we are all the same.

This holds true for us being God. You see, God exists in all things. God gives the fabric and foundation for its existence. At the same token, our soul is a bubble of God and within our soul is God. On the exterior of our soul, we are different but within our bubble, we are the same. This is why the 3rd law of creation states, "The One is All and the All is One." You are a bubble that contains God within you and for that, you are God. You are a creator. Would a creator focus on the lack or would he focus on the abundance? Is God limited? Are you as a soul limited?

When you return back to your immortal self, returning back home, you are not bound by the physical limits nor any limits. You become unlimited and one of the infinite aspects of being human is understanding and realizing once again, the unlimitedness you have. You are abundance and how can abundance ever experience lack or scarcity? It cannot, but it can experience the illusion of scarcity. It can experience the illusion of lack.

For some of you, you may say, "I can look at my bank account right now and no matter how hard I focus or use the words, I don't see a million dollars there." And I agree with you. What you are doing is focusing on a specific point of time right now and looking at your status. But, truth be told, there is trillions of dollars circulating around the world. The total amount of wealth circulating the world is $241 trillion dollars. (Source: https://bit.ly/2ypKfwx). $241 trillion dollars. If you made those 100 dollar bills and stacked them upon one another, you would make it 68% of the distance to the moon. It is unfathomable of how much money exists. And the thing is, most of the individuals with this money, know how to utilize it into their life. If you wanted to get a piece of the market of this, all you have to do is focus and declare what it is you desire. It is as simple as this.
You may experience a lack of abundance when it comes to money, but the only reason why you are experiencing that is due to the words you are choosing and where your focus is at (story/

belief system) on money. If you understood that the Universe works for you, it does so even with money. Hell, money is nothing but life energy. You can only experience more of it if you change the way you view your relationship with money.

Change the way you express money with your words. Change the way you view money with your stories. Change the belief systems you have with money. Here is a list of the top 10 negative belief systems about money

1. ***Money is the root of all evil***
2. ***Money is not that important. It's only money***
3. ***Money is there to be spent***
4. ***The rich get richer and the poor get poorer***
5. ***I'm just not good with money***
6. ***My family has never been rich***
7. ***Money is a limited resource***
8. ***You have to work (too) hard to get wealthy***
9. ***Either rich or happy or either rich or healthy.***
10. ***It's selfish to want a lot of money***

Based on what we have talked about in this book so far, where is the focus of most of this? Do you see a synergistic relationship with what they are saying and the manifesting of money? They are pushing away money in all aspects.

When I was growing up, I was always told #2, #3, #4, #6, #7, #8 and #9. My father would always say, I rather have happiness than be rich. His view on money is, most people who have money have more problems, always stressed out and from what he viewed based upon what he focused on, he saw this often. From Chapter 1 and 2, you know why he saw this all the time. :)

For me, I had to truly break these patterns as I was always hit with these negative belief systems. It happened so many times until one day, I became tired of having these play out in my subconscious mind. The tapes were on replay and the words were being expressed and my focus would go to these places on default until I started to change the story. I started to use words and make sure the words I used were going to declare a different reality than the one I was experiencing.

This took time to manifest and transform, but as I continued to work on my vocabulary and become more aware of what I was telling myself, the stories I believed and what I focused on, I started to slowly mend my life into what I chose to experience. And this was the beginning of a different reality than what I used to experience. The more I focused on this, the more I felt I was breaking through and experiencing what I wanted to experience. I started to step into my power which is source energy and declared a different life. From my word, all things started to shift. In the bible, it talks about this in many different sources:

> **By the word of the LORD, the heavens were made and by the breath of his mouth, all their host.**
>
> *Psalm 33:6*

> **For He spoke, and it was done; He commanded, and it stood fast.**
>
> *Psalm 33:9*

> **But they deliberately overlook the fact that long ago, by God's word, the heavens existed and the earth was formed out of water and by water.**
>
> *2 Peter 3:5*

There are many other verses in the Bible that talk about God's word and how it created the Universe, the heavens and more. But remember, you are a creator and since God exists in all things, God exists in you, which makes you God also. This allows for you to create based upon your word. How you define something, defines the reality of that experience. Whatever you say it is, it shall be. And once you understand this power, you start to take full control of your life and understand how life is more of a game than we think. Imagine if all we had to do is focus on a word that clearly describes what we choose to experience. It would be set in stone and when you are 100% confident to know it will happen regardless of any circumstances that show up, now you are within your power.

What I want you to do right now is take a moment and reflect on your life and feel the areas of your life that you feel like you are creating and what are other areas of your life you feel are happening more to you than for you. Take a moment and write them down.

From there, I want you to focus on next, how to describe each of these. For example, the things that are going well for you, what words do you choose to explain those things? Are they words of a higher vibration like great, amazing, fantastic, etc., or are they words that are lower vibration such as not good, boring, annoyed, etc.?

What you will start to notice is, when you talk about something that you enjoy, you use words that are of a higher vibration. You will notice you feel good when you talk about it. But the opposite is true for you when it comes to talking about the things you dislike. You can tell your energy lowers and you don't feel as great as you did before. Powerful stuff?

But, if you change the words and focus you are using, you can change the entire experience.

For example, this is something I focus on in my office and try to help people understand how health works. In America, as I am writing this book, we are usually dead last or close to when we are compared to the top industrialized nations in health care. Americans consume over 75% of the world's prescription drugs, but only make up 5% of the world's population and we still continue to be one of the unhealthiest countries. Obviously from these states, the current system doesn't work and we are failing miserably at it. Well, let's use what we have learned in this chapter to help explain why this is.

In America, when I am speaking to many people, I will ask a question, "What is health to you?" The most common responses I receive are:

1. Absence of Sickness/illness

2. Feeling good
3. No pain, symptoms or issues
4. Eating well (nutrition)
5. Exercising

These are the most common answers I will receive. And I look at them and say, "They are all good answers, but let us evaluate each of them and see how well they hold up."

For #1-3, have you ever known someone who was doing amazing well, no issues and feeling great and the next week, was diagnosed with cancer, had a heart attack, diagnosed with diabetes, had a stroke, etc.?

For most of us, we either experienced this or know of someone who has. I know I have in all aspects to this. Now, did this just happen out of nowhere or was this something that started a long time ago? Most of the time, people will look and say, it may have started a long time ago. So, if absence of sickness/illness is the indicator of good health, then this is a poor indicator. Feeling good and no pain is another poor indicator. Why?

50% of heart attacks are asymptomatic. 100% of the time, you cannot feel Cancer, Heart Disease, Diabetes, Tooth Decay, Dementia, etc., building up in your body until it has created a lot of damage. Can you see how this is a poor indicator to define health and that, with these definitions, it creates a gamble on our health, never knowing when something may show up or not.

Let us look at the next two, nutrition and exercise. The same question comes up. Have you or someone you know, experienced cancer, heart disease, diabetes, stroke, etc., when they exercised regularly and consumed a healthy diet? I know I can name a few. I had someone who was a second mother to me (I called her my second grandmother) who ate healthy and exercised regularly and ended up battling cancer for 14 years before it was her time. I can go on with many other people who I know have passed who did these things.

James F. Fixx, author of the book, "The Complete Book of Running," died while he was jogging from a heart attack. He was one of the pioneers of jogging and helping in the fitness revolution.

Here was a man who exercised consistently but yet, chronic disease still got to him.

So, there has to be something else that defines health in a better context. Once we discover what that is, we can change our healthcare within a short period of time. Because what you define, becomes your reality. What you define, becomes your experience. So, if more Americans change their definition on health, we can transform our healthcare system. It will not be Obamacare, Trumpcare, anyone's care that will do it. Those systems are dependent upon the first three.

So, what is health then?

Health is all based upon how well your body functions. Diabetes is a sign of the body not functioning well over a long period of time. Heart disease and Cancer are signs of the body not functioning well over a long period of time. Tooth decay is the body not functioning well over a long period of time. I want you to think of it this way.

Imagine you are driving on the road and you end up hitting a big pothole. Now, here in Chicago this can happen often. As you continue to drive, you notice, you can still speed up as fast as you like, brake as hard as you need, turn as much as you have to and go wherever you want to go. To you, the feeling of the car appears to be OK. But what you don't sense and realize is, that pothole ended up shifting your alignment on the car, just so slightly. It is starting to create dysfunction and not be in an optimal state as it was designed to.

As you continue driving, it may take 4 months, 8 months, 12 months, 18 months, 24 months or even longer. Each car is different. But one day, you are driving, enjoying the nice weather with your windows down and you hear a big, "BOOM!" Next thing you know, the car is pulling hard to the right and you slam on the brakes to hopefully slow it down. Once the car comes to a stop, you run out to see what happens and you notice your tire blew out.

You start to ponder and wonder, man, I have bad luck. How could this happen to me? Everything was fine just the day ago and now this? This came out of nowhere! And you start to believe it just happened today. Truth is, this dysfunction happened back when you hit that big pothole. You couldn't sense or notice any difference, but the misalignment caused extra wear and tear on the tire which made it susceptible to blowing out one day. All the added stresses since that pothole only accelerated the process.

When we look at your life, your body is the car. The blown-out tire is any type of condition, illness, symptom or disease that is labeled. We will look at that event and be puzzled as to how this happened, but truth be told, this happened over a period of time. A period of time that was having the body not function at its optimal state. And from there, as life goes on, the accumulation of stress from that point, allowed for this event to take place. It allowed for all the things to add up. This is your KARMA. The Karma as we discussed earlier in the book.

So, if we change our definition to look at how well our body is functioning rather than look at symptoms, we can change healthcare. Because when you look at function, you can find out how much dysfunction is happening in the body and have no symptoms with it, correct it, and help maintain the correction so you can maximize your human potential. This, my friend, is what Chiropractors do on a daily basis. Because the one thing that controls your health and overall function of your body, is your nervous system and Chiropractors are the only professionals out there that analyze for this dysfunction and help make the body become more optimal so you can experience your full human potential and quality of life.

As we define things in our life, it will define our experiences. This is why, when you live by a label and let that label create your identity, you give it so much power, more than you could ever know. It is like putting on a permanent mask and never truly showing the world who you really are. Careful on the words you use to define things. Because those words can truly transform your life.

To share some science to back up how this works even more and how much it affects your life and the people around you. There was a study done by Dr. Masaru Emoto called, "The Water Experiment." In his study, what he wanted to understand was the vibrational effects of words on water. So, what he would do is say the word, "love" and then see how the molecular structure of water would look when frozen. What he found out was mind-blowing.

When he put the word, "love," on water and froze it, when looking under a microscope of the water, it appeared to be in the hexagonal and crystalline form. This is a very high vibrational, healthy form of water alignment. When he used the word, "hate," he noticed after freezing and looking under a microscope, the water had much chaos and was distorted. There was no organization.

Since then, he has tested it out with music, words, water found in nature, photos, prayer and much more. The research and results are amazing, and proof that what we say, and the emotions we use, define our reality. It shows that our consciousness, can truly affect the molecular structure of water and the question is, what does that do to us and our lives since our body is made up of 67%-72% water? How does that affect our energy? Our energy field? Our cellular function? Our health? Life? etc.?

Another great book that breaks this down in a whole different fashion but calls it, "Levels of Consciousness," is a book called, "Power vs Force," by Dr. David Hawkins. This book transformed my life and put things into a perspective I could understand the fabric of life. In this book, he will explain the level of consciousness, from a range of 1 to 1000. He researched this for over 30 years and documented it within his book. From there, he has broken down different emotions, religions, countries, leaders of our world, etc., on where their consciousness levels were. For example, as I talked about in chapter 1, Jesus, Krishna and Buddha, are the three individuals who walked this earth at a consciousness level of 1000. 1000 is the highest level the nervous system can handle. Anything over that, and the body would explode. I kid you not. We are talking about energy here, and your power, your source energy is infinite. This is why you don't take your body with you. Your physical body cannot hold onto the high vibrational fields. Just like the mind does not see all perspectives but only a few. Just like you can only truly focus on one thing at one time. Multi-tasking is truly an illusion. Sorry folks! Anyhow, I recommend this book to you because it truly can take things deeper and have you understand the words you use and how they play a role in your life.

It's important to be careful of the words we use for those words and how we use them, will indefinitely, define your life. Change your words, change your vocabulary, and you will change your life. It is that simple. We will dive more into this in the next couple chapters, but for now, let me share a story on how a word I used all the time, pulled me away from what I chose to experience.

In my life, I played many sports and was very competitive. My competition was not with others but more with testing myself. I would see who was the best in the league and then, set my standards to being at that level as a minimum. This has helped me thrive in sports, especially in my late teens, early 20s. I have taken this mentality in my life to business and achieving the vision and legacy I want to leave on this planet. I truly believe we are all here to share a part of our light with this world, with humanity and help it at a higher vibration than what it was when we first entered it.

In this process of always striving to grow and become better, I would say to myself, "I need to push myself through this." When I would train, I would get exhausted but then say, "I need to push through. There will be time for rest but not now." And I would continue to do this through all things. When I was in outpatient clinic in Chiropractic school, I sought out to finish early. I wanted to go home for 2-3 months and be able to spend time with family and start my vision of what I wanted to create in my office and becoming a chiropractor and leader of my community.

After 2 months in outpatient clinic, I did not have many patients. The successes I thought I would have were not happening. I kept pushing harder, marketing, talking with people in grocery stores and so much more. I thought I had to push harder to strive and hit my goals. Heck, all my mentors talked about the hustle and the grind. How I had to always work harder than the competition or else, I wouldn't achieve the results I desired. Again, what you define becomes your reality. How do you think my reality became?

I will never forget this day. It was the end of November and I was talking on the phone with my mom and I was having a bad day. I told her that I was not achieving the results I thought I would have and I started to judge myself as thinking I wasn't good enough or this was the right fit for me. My mother just said, "Give it time. It will all work out." After a couple days, I started to change the words from push and grind to achieve my goals to saying to myself, "It will be done. I am going to experience X and it has already been done." I started to stop using the word, push, hustle, grind and started to use the word, "in flow and trusting the Universe." Long story short, 2-3 months afterwards, I had so many new patients, my staff doctor thought I was paying people to be a patient of mine. Before you know it, by May, I was able to leave and had finished up all my required adjustments and much more.

It was a moment in time that, once I changed my words, my life in front of me changed. I actually worked way less than normal and was achieving the results that I desired. This is called, "The Path of Least Resistance." We will cover this in much depth in the upcoming chapters. So, don't jump ahead. Everything I am sharing with you is a building block from one thing to the next.

So, this is a great time to see how you define things. How do you define your health? Your relationships? Your Friends? Your family? Your mental health? Your physical health? Your spiritual life? Your career/business?

Take 5-10 minutes and just reflect on the words you currently use. One way to know if you are choosing words of empowerment is by looking at these areas of your life and seeing which ones are doing very well and which ones are not. Usually, the ones that are not, are because of the choice of words one uses. You see, Karma means action and it is the accumulation of action that leads to where you are right now. Karma is also the accumulation of your words and how often you repeat them that reinforce your reality and experience of now.

The reason why words are so critical for creating your reality is because as we talked about in the past chapter, words are the things you focus on. When you choose words to describe or define something, it is like choosing a movie or show on Netflix, Hulu or any other On-Demand programs. It is creating the experience of what it is you desire.

Let us use an example of how this defines individuals in our lives. Is there someone in the world, in your life, that you dislike? For some reason, you just dislike the person no matter what? No matter what they say, do or act, you will find a reason to dislike them? We all have them in our lives. Even I do and I will try to adjust and shift my focus as much as I can.

Haven't you noticed, the person who you dislike, no matter what, you find the things that you describe in words? For example, if you dislike this person because they are annoying. The word, annoying, is how you define them. What will your experience always be? This person is annoying regardless of what that person does.

When you define someone, you put them in a box. When you define anything in this world, you choose what you want to focus on and disregard the rest. This is the same thing as we discussed when it comes to the honeymoon state of a relationship.

Have you ever found someone in your life who you think is hilarious and funny? Do you catch yourself laughing at almost anything they say? Why is that? Is it because they are funny? Probably and your experiences of what you focused on showed that. But, what if you find them to be annoying. Will they still be funny? Probably not. This is the power you have over your experience. You can choose whatever experience you want to have. Life is all about the perspective and your words can help you focus deeper on things to create a more fulfilling and enriched life.

I want to share with you why most people who grow up in families have very similar experiences as others. Why is it that, if you come from a family that can barely make ends meet and has a negative belief system with money, most of the family members do not achieve much success? It is the words that they use to allow for them to be their language. And what happens when you choose the same words as your family members? Most of the time, you will experience the same things they do, but just different with the times. So, how can you break away from this prison? Change your vocabulary.

I come from a family of blue collar workers. My father laid carpet for a living while working a full-time job at a grocery store warehouse. My mother was a fitness/yoga instructor and she also was a nail technician. They worked endless hours to provide for my sister and I. I didn't have a lot, but my parents did the best they could and it is all I would have ever asked. From this point on in my life, I have learned how to appreciate everything in life because, growing up, we didn't have everything. For us, it was one good thing and that was it. I remember I wanted to get a Super Nintendo, and I told my mom I was going to buy it because I knew they couldn't get it for me at that time. I waited patiently, focused on what I wanted, pictured myself playing games on there and so forth. Within 6 months, I had the money to buy the entire console and a couple games. :)

What words did I use? How did I manifest that? I kept telling myself, "I will have a SuperNintendo." I didn't leave the door open for any doubt, worry, or fear. I stated, "It will happen."

So, how do you break away from the programming of family? Choose different words. If you continue to focus on this and do the work, I can promise you, you will have a different experience. It is a Universal law. I am not the one who made this up. I discovered what this was and how to utilize it in my life.

Your word is what sets the tone of creation. From word, comes the experience. For all things to have existed in the physical world, it all started from a word. That word has defined the constructs of that physical existence and from that, the experience was created. You can take this on a global perspective. You can take this on a specific country, village, state, etc. How you define it will be. The more people who define something in a specific way, the more it becomes our reality. It becomes more of the human experience.

For example, when I say the word, "Terriorist," what do you see in your head? What words, culture, religions comes to mind? The ones you think of are the ones you have used and created. They are the ones you have been conditioned to think, believe and see a certain way. If I say the word, "Donald Trump," you have a specific reaction to it. It is all based upon the words you use to define this person. This is the same thing for anything else in life. And the beauty of this is, you can see how you define something and start to realize that, when you define it, you give it your power, and this power comes from your Source Energy. Source energy is the fabric of who you really are and what we are all made of. Source energy is God and God is in all things. So, when you come from Source Energy, that is the Creator of all things and you are a creator of all things.

You create through your words. Your words and what you allow to be utilized as your words will create the reality of what you are experiencing. If you are experiencing something that is not what you have chosen, always know, you are constantly choosing and it may be something that you are focusing on that is pulling you away from your vision. Look at the words you use and how you define them. Most of the time, it is there. At least, that is the beginning.

Remember in the 5 laws of Creation, one of them stated, "What you put out in the Universe comes back to you." What words you use will come back to you in your experience. The Universe is always responding to what you put out there. It is always serving you to help give to you what you choose to experience. You are the one who chooses your experiences and using words plays a huge role in how that experience is manifested.

I want you to think of the words you use as the tools and equipment you have to build your house. Your house is a result of the words you use. When we think of words, it will be the materials that you use. And the materials are all based upon how well of a word you use. For example, do you believe that the words, good vs. great vs. epic vs. amazing, have different feelings and different results? I would say so. I love using the word, fantastic, and the more I use it, the more I can see how that plays a role in my life. I am not saying I feel that way all the time. The truth is I don't. But I choose to set the stage as much as I can so that, 95% of the time, I do feel that way. I am human and being perfect is not a human trait. We are all flawed and we all make mistakes, but through our imperfections, it is what makes us perfect for whatever we choose to do. :)

So, as you define different aspects of your house with your words, the quality of materials and tools will be utilized in this house. You will start to notice that, in some parts of your house, you had the best materials and tools that this Universe could provide and then, there will be parts of your house where the materials were mediocre or under average. No matter how much you enter the part of your house that is mediocre, it will not change, unless you change the words on how you describe and define that part of your life. From there, you can slowly change that part of the house with better materials and tools. And slowly but surely, it will manifest into what it is you chose to experience.

Always remember, the Universe is working FOR you, not AGAINST you. If you don't like what you are experiencing in your life, change your focus, change the way you define and express it and watch how it will slowly transform. Remember, we live in a Space Time continuum, which means it takes time and some space for you to experience what you chose. But to get things moving in that direction happens instantaneously.

Chapter 4

We Are All Interdependent

**When you focus on being your best, everyone wins....
When you are less than your best, only a very few truly
are able to experience the amazing light you are...**

Dr. Vic Manzo Jr.

As we discussed about when you are your best, everyone wins, and when you are not, it is very few who see the greatness. When I was coming out of Chiropractic school, I had a mentality of saving the world. I took this to an extreme. I would stay up long days, studying the greatest millionaires, billionaires and saw what they did to become successful. I started reading more about the philosophy of Chiropractic, Universal Laws, Quantum Physics and wanted to know the depths of what is the fabric to healing. I would listen to YouTube videos on motivation, inspiration, how to break through your barriers and so much more, every single day. I wouldn't stop and I wouldn't stop. I knew what I had chosen to do and wanted to do and was going to do all that I could to learn from the best so I could be the best. I was creating this formula that, as long as I did X, Y, Z, I would end up seeing the results I desired.

As I kept pushing and grinding, as I kept hustling and learning, I would have a faint voice every once in a while within me say, get centered. Get calm. You are working too hard and not efficient. But, I kept saying, "It is what I do behind closed doors that creates the growth for who and what I desire." I created a podcast and did over 100 shows within 2 years. I wrote many blogs, posted endlessly on social media about information regarding health and educate the hell out of my patients about their human body, how the body works and the more they understand what health is, the more I am able to empower them to choose the health they desire.

You can see, this was a lot of work and I would be seriously doing this for 9-12 hours a day, 4-5 days a week. I was hungry as they say. I had a hunger that never went away. I had a thirst for knowledge, wisdom and inspiration.

I would sign up for different online programs, seminars, workshops to just learn what was out there and learn what I could do to help and do more. As I kept doing this, I felt that I needed to continue doing these things so I could be an amazing Doctor, a life transformational trainer and truly guide people towards the life they desired through health via Chiropractic.

Boy, did I find out later, I was wrong. The thing was, I was never fulfilled. I started to realize that, there are universal laws that talk about this. I kept putting endless energy out into the Universe thinking that, as long as I put out there, the ripple effects will come back to me. What ended up happening is, I started to realize I was doing the complete opposite. I was pushing the things I actually wanted in my life.

In this chapter, we will talk about this amazing and powerful Universal law called, "The Universal Law of Vibration/Manifestation/Attraction." And through this law, I started to realize that all I wanted to achieve, all I wanted to become, was not outside of me, but within me. I started to see that, in order to add to the world, I had to leave a legacy and leave this place better than when I first came here, I needed to focus strictly on me. It was a moment in time when I started to truly understand that, all the answers reside within you. All you need to do is trust the flow and know it will be what you chose.

In order to understand the truth on the Law of Vibration, one has to understand that, we as humans, collectively, create a vibration, a consciousness. This consciousness is the experience of what we have on this planet. And when we average out every single human being, measure their thoughts, emotions, well-being, energy, etc., it will come out as a number based upon their consciousness levels overall. In the book, "Power vs Force," by Dr. David Hawkins, he explains much more in depth on how this works and how it is evaluated.

For this chapter, I want you to think of the concept that, the higher the level of consciousness, the more experiences of love exist in your world and the lower the level of consciousness, the more fear you experience in your world.

So, each person has a range of where they are at, and when we add up all the humans, it gives us a concept of our experience. The collective consciousness is what creates the majority of the experiences of this world. When we talked about focus in Chapter two and the power behind it, we are looking at focus on a macro level. We are looking at what are the majority of human's focusing on. What are the things they are choosing, believing in, their rituals, habits, etc. All these accumulative choices from all humans create the foundation for the human experience.

Now, just like any great human mind would do, we love logic and compartmentalizing things. So, you can break it down into continents like North America, South America, Asia, etc. You can break it down to the United States, Italy, Spain, Russia, New Zealand, etc. You can take it further down into the micro level of Chicago, London, Hong Kong, Sydney, etc. You can go further and pick smaller towns and you can go further into family units. And then, you go to the most basic unit, which happens to be YOU. You are the most basic unit of the collective consciousness, but don't let the size fool you. You play an unbelievable role in the entire consciousness.

This was something that took me years to experience even though I knew the concept of it. I have learned through the time I have spent here, it is the experiences that will always overpower the knowledge of things.

So, as I looked at my life and all that I was doing to make the world the best place ever, I was missing the biggest link to doing that.

> **"You must be the change you want to see in the world."**
> *Gandhi*

It is amazing how, I have read this quote so much that one day, it clicked. In order to see the world become better, it is not what you do that will make the world better, it is who you are that makes the world better. It is the growth, expansion, evolutionary process of who you are that raises the vibration of this world. It is from this, that you are able to transform it and improve upon it. All things start with you and only you. This is true only for you.

Together, we are all playing in this game called, "Life," and what we do in this life, affects every single other person, whether they are conscious or not. For fear to exist, we all must believe in fear and focus on it. In order for tyrants to exists, we must allow fear to exist within our hearts for that is what we focus on. In order for terrorists to exist, we focus on lower vibrational thoughts and emotions that allow for the things we see in the world happen.

I was reading a blog on www.ErikChanneling.com and the question came up, why are we seeing so much terror attacks, mass shootings and much more happening in the world? What Erik explained was brilliant. He stated, "When majority of humans start to appreciate life and respect life, there will be no need for terrorist attacks. But until we, as humans, learn this lesson, we will continue to see this happen regardless of what efforts we do to stop it."

For some of you, you may feel that, this is too much out of control or nonsense, but you have to understand this one principle: Law of Vibration. The Law of Vibration works on so many levels and right now, we are talking about it in the form of experiences in life. How we, all play and work together to create an experience, called Life. It is we, who create our experiences as a whole. The micro is just as important as the macro.

When you start to truly see the big picture on this, now things start to become fun. You start to realize, you can shape your world with your own thoughts and emotions. You have the power to make the shift and start focusing on what it is you desire. Once you start to do that, everything will start to shift and change. But it all starts with you. You have the power. You are as just as important the whole as much as you are the part.

Now, some may ask, what keeps the consciousness levels where they are? How are they affected? How are the experiences manipulated or programed a specific way? This is the part that I have heard so many times that I will explain in full detail.

The good thing out of all of this, is that you have the power to make the change and become the shift. You start to become the change in the world that you desire. This is why it is so important to focus on you and only you. You are the only person you can control. You can control your attitude, your emotions, your reactions to life and much more. This all plays a role on the level of consciousness you are choosing and experiencing. What I was doing, when I first came out of Chiropractic school was, trying to make the change in others and influence them which in return, I felt would have helped empower the world, but as you can see, that was a flawed idea. I would rather say, a path that I would never end up achieving.

Why would it be a path I would never achieve?

The truth is, there is a machine that is constantly programming our minds, our thoughts, our emotions to have us believe a reality that is not one of your own. There is a programming that happens on so many levels that it is starting to isolate us more than ever before and control our minds without us even knowing it.

The sad thing is, television, the news, shows movies, radio shows, podcasts, books you read, magazines you read, and people you follow are all programming your mind, and the key thing is, the more people who believe in these things, the more it holds ground and becomes a reality. The more you associate yourself with these things, the more it becomes who you are and sets the stage for your level of vibration. It programs us to believe something so deep, that it makes us believe it was our own idea in the first place. So many people in the world, are wearing a mask, thinking it's truly who they are, but in reality, it is not.

Some people will take offense to what I said, but remember in Chapter 1, I talked about the labels that make up who you are. But in reality, you are neither the labels nor are you the titles. The labels and titles are just the mask covering up the truth of who you are and the main message I want to share with you is to help you realize the truth of who you are, understand the game of Life so you can choose a more fulfilled and inspiring life so that it will help liberate others to experience the same thing.

The problem with today's information era is that, we are bombarded with information all the time and the more and more we see the same type of information that exists, we start to believe it to be true. Heck, there is even something that many follow in the media world. Joseph Goebbels, Hitler's right hand man, who led the propaganda in Germany stated, "If you say a lie loud enough and long enough, people will start to believe it." I am not saying that the mainstream media lies. What I will say is, they will contort stories to sell the negativity. Unfortunately in that world, negativity sells and the more you can slander someone, destroy someone, publicly humiliate someone, that is good news and people love to hear these types of things.

Repetition is the mother of all learning, and the more things are repeated, shared and expressed, the more it is ingrained into their consciousness, which creates the consciousness of a state, a country and eventually, the world.
You can look at this concept in all aspects of life for you will find it there. This law works upon animals, insects, humans, plants, trees, etc. It affects every life forms on this planet. It is a program, a conditioning that happens. The more it is repeated, the more it becomes ingrained within.

Let us look at Cancer. God forbid, if you or someone you know experiences cancer, what are the treatment options? Most people will say, chemotherapy, radiation and surgery. Are there any other options out there?

Based upon the medical world, there is not. Based upon their power of influence through the years, people believe that is all there is also. But, the fact is, there are other options that are not treatments as described by the medical model but instead, focus on how to repair the body to become optimal again. And when you work on helping the body to become optimal, is there room for cancer? If you are 100% healthy, is there room for disease? Different types of concept. Instead of dumping massive toxins into the body (chemotherapy) to kill off the cancer and weaken other parts of the body, how about work with repairing the body and giving it what it needs? What if that changes the course?

The reason why we are so stuck on believing that Cancer can only be cured through chemotherapy, radiation and/or surgery is because we have been told this for so long. We have been told this over many years and now, there is endless information about cancer, chemotherapy treatments and much more. There are tons of races, months, days, etc., dedicated to this. We have hardwired it into our consciousness that, when it comes to Cancer, chemotherapy, radiation and surgery is the answer and if I pass the 5-year mark, I am a Cancer survivor. We have been programmed to think that we need to fight this cancer in order to win. I have seen so many people use the term, I am a fighter and I never give up. My question is, "What are you fighting for?" You are not fighting for your life if you are life. You are not fighting the cancer because the body made the cancer so are you fighting your body? Why would the body create something like this?

This is one of the biggest programs we have believed and given into and to be honest, it's easy, because when a doctor states, "You have cancer," your mind goes immediately into fear mode, and when you are in a state of fear, you cannot think critically clear. Your decision making process goes out the door. From there, you just choose whatever is going to be survival most of the time and rarely a state of thriving.

This is the concept that we face on a daily basis and it is up to us, on what we associate with that will truly shape our reality.

Mother Theresa always said, "I would never go to an anti-war rally. I would always go to a peace rally." Can you see the difference between the two? An anti-war rally's focus is on the war. What happens when you focus on something? You give it power.

Hence, she rather focuses on a peace rally because she is giving Peace the power.

During the 2016 US Presidential Elections, Donald Trump used this to his advantage. The more he can get people to talk about him, the more his name was being used. The more people can associate from one to the other. I am not saying this is why he won or anything political. I am just using this as an example of what we are talking about today. But the Law of Association sits true here also.

When I say Donald Trump, what comes to mind? What do you think of? Some of you will choose nice thoughts, while some will choose negative. Here is a question, out of all the slanders that have gone on in the media, my question to you is, have you ever sat down and hung out with Donald Trump, not once, but multiple times? Do you know who he truly is on the inside? Most people haven't and we assume what the news tells us, will construe in a way to make us believe it based upon what they want you to believe.

Let us take the attention away from Donald Trump as I know this brings up a lot of emotions for people. Let me take this to a different aspect: Chiropractic and children receiving Chiropractic care. What if I said, it is imperative for an infant to be checked by a Chiropractic immediately after being born. How many people see the purpose behind this? How many people think it's crazy? Regardless of what you think, it is all based upon what you associate yourself with on a common basis. It is what you have been told over many times or have seen or have experienced that will sway you towards one or not.

The truth is, what you listen to, read, spend your time with, watch, and talk about are all framing your reality and your experiences. The more you are exposed to something, the more you believe it to be true. This can be in every aspect of your life. If you think life is supposed to be a certain way, good chance it may be a programming or condition you developed over time and not truly what you feel is true.

Here is a great test to understand how this works. The Law of Association states you are what you associate yourself with the most. I want you to take the 5 closest people you spend the most time with (adults) and when you average them out, that is you. As this works on a human collective consciousness level, this also works on families and friends. Have you ever noticed you are not super close to everyone in your family but just a handful or so. It all comes down to the law of association.

So with this law, what can we do? What can we transform? As Gandhi stated, "It all starts from one." And it starts with you. No matter what happens in the world, you can be the change in the world. All you need to do is focus on it. Focus on what you want to do and just do it. Simple, right?
At least that is how it is supposed to be. Life was never designed to be this complicated and you would think with technology, it would make things easier for us, but it has created a more complex world. Here is an example on health.

When it comes to our health, we believe that it has to be a complex solution to a complex problem. When I communicate with potential patients and educate on how the nervous system controls every single function and cell within your body, that once we clear the miscommunications, the body will restore itself back to its optimal potential. Simple. But it gets even simpler. When patients come in for an adjustment, they are amazed at how quick the adjustment is. I will spend 2-3 minutes with a patient. That is all that is needed to find and adjust a subluxation (miscommunication/interference within the nervous system).
Once I make my adjustments, the work begins. It is a very simple process that allows for your body to restore itself back to its natural design. It allows for your source energy/intelligence to flow better and when these things are slowly starting to happen, you experience maximized human potential.

But, the complex world we live in, many people will say, "This simple procedure cannot be the solution to what I have going on?" I will always reiterate that Chiropractic does not treat or cure any condition, illness or disease. What it is designed to do is help people experience their maximized human potential. That is it.

What happens over a period of weeks to months is, with no other changes in their life, they notice how things start to get better but not just their symptoms. They start to notice other things like more energy, better sleep, better mood, calmer, not so stressed out, level-headed, improved performance, improved attitude, better focus and concentration and much more. What I love is people will still be in shock that just a simple adjustment does that. I will tell them, "I felt the same way when my Chiropractor first told me the story also. I couldn't believe how a simple adjustment would change all of this and it did. It transformed my life so much; it is like I am a completely different person, more connected to my source."

We can simplify all the causes of diseases, illnesses and conditions into two categories: Deficiency and Toxicity. Once we find the deficiency and the toxicities to the body and start to help the body repair and heal, health can exist. It is as simple as this. But, our current medical systems have complicated things to show how complex the body is. Chiropractors, we understand the complexity of the body and how it creates a miracle every single day. Our goal is to express that miracle more and more. And once we do, we know for a fact, maximized human potential can be experienced.

So, how do we pull away from the programming of the collective consciousness of humanity? How can we truly start to create our own program and be the change we desire to see in the world? Simple. Focus on what it is you want and don't lose sight of it. Whatever that may be. Just focus on it.

When I was 7 years old, I had a medical doctor tell my mother that I would not be able to play any sports when I was in high school and by the time I was the age of 30 years old, I would need to have a hip replacement. Being a kid at 7 years old who loved to play sports, this was not the brightest day of my life. I could have let the doctor, who was stating something that the medical system believes to be true; it is their collective consciousness that when something happens in your life, here is the one-track way of what you will experience. Think about that for a second. If you have cancer, what is your experience going to be? When you have heart disease, what is your experience going to be? When you have diabetes, what is your experience going to be? The collective consciousness of the medical system of today is, drugs, injections and surgery. That is their tool box and all that they know. I am not saying this is bad by any means, but what I am saying is, this is the collective consciousness of it. It is neither good nor bad, it just is.

So, what the doctor was saying was based upon the collective consciousness of the medical system, but I was not going to have any of that. I was depressed that day, but I knew I was going to prove him wrong. So, I started to focus on myself and playing sports. I kept focusing on how I can get better, stronger and faster. I started to see myself playing sports all the time. Since I was so hyper-focused and tuned in, what do you think happen?

Just like picking a show out on Netflix/Hulu, I picked the experience of playing sports and I did just that. I played organized soccer and baseball. I played tackle football almost weekly with my friends. I played basketball almost daily. I will never forget, my parents bought me a basketball rim to put outside in our driveway. In the summer, I would go out almost every day to play and my house became the hangout for playing basketball. We would play all day. When I reached high school, I took it to another level.

I still played soccer and baseball on the high school level, but played tackle football on the weekends and then basketball and racquetball 3-4 days a week with friends. I just loved to play sports and what the sports taught me about life.

Long story short, when I was 31 years old, I took an x-ray of my hips to see if there was any sign of degeneration or need of surgery. Don't be shocked, but my hips are perfectly clear of any signs of degeneration and from a chiropractic standpoint, very well-balanced, especially for the scoliosis I have.

You see, the moral of the story is, whatever you choose to experience, just focus on what it is you desire and you have to do this daily. Because when you don't do this, you end up allowing for the collective to take over.

A great quote I used to say, but don't recall who said it. "If you don't choose what to experience each day, the world will do it for you."

What are you choosing every day? Are you setting up your game plan for the day? Remember, the collective is always working against you. The collective consciousness is not something that is designed to bring you to your best. Actually, it is the opposite. The collective consciousness of humanity or any country, state, town, is all about being average or mediocre. If you don't focus on what it is you choose to experience daily, you will start to lead towards an average life.

And again, I am not saying average is bad or good. It just is. And if you want to be like everyone else, hell, be that! There is nothing wrong with that. We are all on our own journey in this life to gain an experience we call, "Human being." There is no right or wrong. There just is. So, whatever that experience is you want to have, go for it. The purpose of this book is to help you lead a fulfilled and inspired life. A fulfilled and inspired life is all based upon what you see that is. For some, it can be watching 2 hours of TV per night. For some, it can be binge watching shows on Netflix. For some, it is reading 100 books a year and trying to be the best they can.

The beautiful thing about this experience called, "Life," is that there is no right or wrong. The rights and wrongs only exist for the ones who push them upon another. And guess what, those rights and wrongs only exist based upon, you guessed it, a collective consciousness of people thinking what right and wrong should be. Welcome to democracy and our law system in America.

So, you have the power to transform your life, but you have to make sure you are always working on this because when you don't, the collective is. This is what I like to call, "The Machine." The machine is what and where we are all the time as a collective. Google is a great way to see where we are as a collective. The best, in my opinion, is to type words in Google Images and see what is the most common that pop up. From there, this is where you will see where the most of us spend our focus on. It is amazing what shows up and gives you an idea of where we are.

This is a great way to see what we are doing, what we are focusing on and what we, as a collective, are creating in this game called, "LIFE."

Another way to see what we are doing is, just look up the most common Google searches and you will be amazed at what you see. Again, it is another way for us to see what is the most of what we are focusing on. Facebook is another way of seeing what you are focusing on. Are you not amazed that, when you look up something on the internet and then, jump on Facebook or other social media outlets and see what you were looking up? Some say this is control and trying to tap into your head, which it is! But, it is another way to show you, what you focus on, becomes your reality.

So, the truth is, you must be consistent with your focus, every single day, in order to transform your world to what you desire. Keep whatever it is you choose to experience and keep the end in mind. What I mean by end in mind is, "The vision." What is the vision of what you want to achieve?

For me, when I first opened up my office, I had a vision of being the community leader of Wellness in my area. I wanted people, that when they thought of wellness and what it takes to achieve maximized human potential, I was their guy. I was the first person to contact.

Every day, I focus on that vision becoming a reality. And it is OK if the vision changes over time, that means you are evolving. For me, my vision has changed. Now, my vision is seeing moms start their planning stages of having a baby, first get checked and adjusted. To make sure their nervous system is communicating clearly without any interference. This would be for their husband/partner also. From there, moms would be checked and adjusted throughout pregnancy. And then, when the baby is born, have them checked to make sure they have no nerve interference and for that baby to grow and develop the way they were designed to so they are never off-track of their path of living their maximized human potential.

Imagine the kind of world we would have, if children, from a neurological perspective, were living their maximized human potential, from day 1, how different would the world be? How much healthier? We would shift the consciousness and elevate the collective to higher levels of vibrations. We all, would have a different experience of life and slowly reconnect ourselves back to our source which is your TRUE self! How powerful is that? How much of an impact would that make on humanity?

So, when we talk about breaking away from the collective to create a new experience, I want to share with you a story on how this works and how this programming really does exist. The Law of Association is as real as the Law of Gravity. Whether you believe in gravity or not, it exists.

Back in Oxford, England in 1954, there was a gentleman named, "Roger Bannister." He was a medical student who was attempting to beat the 4-minute mile barrier that at this time, no human being had done before. Many people stated it could never be done and many people of this time, attempted to beat the 4-minute mile and it was never completed. As many people kept attempting, it never had been accomplished.

Until one day in 1954, Roger Bannister was running against his Alma Mater, Oxford University, as he represented the Amateur Athletic Association. During that race, he was running the mile and ended up breaking the 4-minute mile run. On record, he ended up achieving 3 minutes and 59.4 seconds. This was the first time ever recorded and performed by a human being. Before this, it was all believed to be insane and never could be possible. Most people believed that to be true and I personally believe this is why many of them failed at it. But Roger Bannister had a different concept within him and knew it could be done if he continued to practice at it. He kept his focus on the prize regardless of what people said (the machine) and was going to pursue this feat which he did accomplish.

Since that time, there have been thousands of people who have performed a sub 4-minute mile run. There are even high school students who are performing this now. But the key thing was, it had to start from someone, something. Someone had to break the barrier of the consciousness level. Someone had to show, it is possible. And from there, as they started to create the change they wanted to see in the world by being a model of it rather than forcing the change, many people were able to break the feat just like he did.

In sports and life, records are meant to be broken. As you have learned in this chapter, a record is broken when someone breaks from the mold, focuses on the prize, creates their own law of association of books, podcasts, videos, coaches, and more to help push them to their limits to one day, they may break that limit. One of the most iconic individuals at this time of writing this book is Usain Bolt and Michael Phelps. Do you think these individuals are talented and this is why they win and break all these records? What do you think it is?

I personally believe based upon what we shared in this chapter, these individuals have a hyper-focus ability to see the prize in mind and know where they want to be. I am not saying these two individuals are amazing, talented and skillful at what they do, which they are. But everything starts within the mind. Things will start and end within the mind first before ever existing onto the physical plane/reality. Nothing can ever escape this. Who you are, the physical being, the label, was created from the mind first, before it became physical. Everything we see, follows this law.

These individuals know how to focus and strive. They don't let the collective, the noise, get in their way. You will see, when they are interviewed, sometimes the questions asked, are a way to get them off focus. They don't let anything get to them, no excuses, no stories, virtually nothing. All the excuses and stories are the collective speaking to you. It is allowing the collective to share their experiences with you and that is what will determine if you succeed or not. Hell, we all have stories. Human beings are the best storytellers. We all put a story to something.

My challenge to you is, are you allowing the stories and voices of the machine affect what you choose to experience? Are you allowing it to push you away from your source, your focus?

There is a beauty when you start to truly focus on YOU. There is something magical that happens to where you start to shift and change to create your own ripple in the ocean of infinite potential.

"Be the change you want to see in the world."

Gandhi

As I stated earlier, this is one of my favorite quotes in life. When you focus on your own vibration and energy and start to pull away from the machine, you give others the opportunity to do the same thing. Whatever you do in your life, gives others the opportunity to do the same thing. We are all interconnected. Being human gives us the illusion that we are separated from one another.

I have my body, you have yours, we are separate. But the truth is, we are all interdependent upon one another. Everything in this world is interdependent upon one another. If you don't believe me, take a look at the global banking system. If one area fails, they all fail. All the banking systems are interdependent upon one another. When it comes to your body, every single hormone is interdependent upon one another. Every single cell is interdependent upon one another. When it comes to sport teams, they are all interdependent on one another. Just because a team has the best player ever in the history of the game, does not make the team great. When all the players are working in a synergistic way, this is how the team becomes great. They are interdependent upon one another.

So, even though, I live in this bubble called, "the human body," and so do you, we are connected in more ways than one. Just like the internet exists that allows for us to connect to anyone, anywhere in the world, there is an internet that connects all of us together called, "The Universe." Some call this God. Some call this Source Energy or Prime Source or Prime Creator. It is this Source that connects all of us. So, what we do in our life, allows for another to do the same.
I was reading and listening to something when Barrack Obama came on and was talking about how, what John Lewis did back in his day and all the work he has done, made it possible for him to

be president and carry the torch per say. It gave Barrack Obama the opportunity to be America's First African American President.

Now, if you don't like this example, here is another one. Back in the 1930s - 1950s, the medical establishment and the government were arresting Chiropractors at that time for, "Practicing medicine without a license." At that time, there was an attack on the profession to eliminate the profession at all costs. It was the biggest threat to the medical establishment. The chiropractor who was put in jail more times than any other chiropractor, Herbert Ross Reaver, stated that, "It was a matter of principle for all of us. We don't practice medicine in any shape or form. To be designated as limited medical practitioners was something intolerable to us. And, of course, it was a useless thing anyway because the so-called permit limited the types of cases we could handle. It was just something that any chiropractor with any guts could not accept." (Source: Bower N, Hynes R Jr. "Going to Jail for Chiropractic: A Career's Defining Moment." Chiropractic History, 2004;24(2):21-26.)

If it wasn't for all the chiropractors who fought for our profession, being put in jail and some of them serving 500-day sentences, I would not be able to do what I am doing today. I would not be able to open up a business, practice chiropractic and serve the masses. Everything we do in our life, sets the stage for the next generation and so forth.

A poem I recommend checking out is Marianne William's poem titled, "Our Deepest Fear." In this poem, she describes how it is up to us to let our own light shine in order for others to do the same. It is through us that we liberate others to do the same thing.

It truly focuses on what it is you want to choose to experience and stay laser focused, you can transform your life and also, give the opportunity for another to do the same. This is not just in sports, chiropractic, running, but in the opportunity for others to experience the power of returning back to their greatness. Understand the game, the laws and realizing how to use them to choose the experiences they desire. It is all summed up right there. This entire poem is designed based around that.

I wasn't given a golden spoon. I didn't have rich parents. I didn't have a great set of positive belief systems. But, all the experiences I went through in life, taught me so much that, I wanted to help others learn what I have learned to be true. I seeked out for a common ground that I can share. Something that, regardless of belief systems and whatnot, you can utilize in your life to help transform it.

I am a work in progress and always will be. And so are you! But, understanding this concept can truly transform your life and help others do the same thing. My parents taught me things their parents couldn't teach them or shared from their experiences. From there, I took them, built upon them and helped create my own world because at the end of the day, what you really are, is a small universe, that is in a cycle of everlasting growth, expansion and evolution.

So, focus on the choices of what you want to experience today, focus on them and make sure to not let the distractions get in the way. Because today, this is even more important than it has ever been due to the information era. And remember what you do in your life, helps others to experience the same. And from you, we can create a new experience for this world. I won't say better, because that is different for each of us. But what I will say, is a higher level of consciousness experience. A higher level up the meter of love. To allow for all of us to experience more love in our hearts, our minds and our world.

Chapter 5

Free Will is Your Spiritual Birthright

"You are not IN the Universe, you ARE the Universe, an intrinsic part of it. Ultimately, you are not a person, but a focal point where the Universe is becoming conscious of itself. What an amazing miracle."

Eckhart Tolle

As we discussed in chapter 1, you are God. You are an integral part of being God. You are part of the infinite souls who are helping God become more conscious of Itself. How powerful if that? How can you have self-worth issues or a self-esteem issue when you truly know who you really are?

Some people get caught up when I say, "You are God." They will allow their preconditioned thinking of the collective consciousness they've chosen to be a part of and accept to set their life think, it is impossible. Know this.

NOTHING exists without GOD. God is all things. As they say, "God is All That Is." You were a creation from God which makes you God. How is this true? Well, you wouldn't be reading this book if it wasn't. Why would you need to create and experience a human life if it was meaningless? What would we need to learn, expand, evolve into if we were all-knowing and knew all things? Experience is the king/queen of all learning. You can know things in life, but when you experience them, that is where the magic is.

Have you ever thought you knew something until one day, had an experience that was totally different than what you thought it would be? I believe we all have. This is the essence of God. To experience and become conscious of Itself because all-knowing is not fun enough.

Imagine having a child and you knew every step of the way they were going to live their life, the experiences, the situations and so forth. You knew exactly what they would say at every moment and knew every emotion they would experience overall. How fun of a life would that be? Would there be much growth in that? Probably not.

I hope you can see the connection here a bit more. Basically, this is a micro-macro view of things. God is the macro view and we are the micro view.

Another way to look at it as looking at a picture. When you look at a picture, you look and it appears that the picture is all, clear colors, borders, etc. But, if you zoom in and continue to zoom in, you will find out it is small singular pixels. When you put these pixels together, they start to form a picture, and the more you zoom out, the more you can see the picture. Well, when we zoom out as far as we can, there is God. Then, when we zoom really far in, we see you and all the other souls around you that make up God.

For a great book that breaks all of this down in much depth is a book called, "Conversations with God," by Neale Donald. Walsch. I highly recommend it. This is one of the most important books I have ever read. It summed up a lot of my meditations, insights and much more. And the cool part is, whenever I am in a tough time in life, feeling hopeless, I will look up and say, "Show me what I need to see." When I open up the book, I have never, I repeat, never have been disappointed.

So, since we dove in during Chapter one about the fabric of who you are: endless, timeless, spaceless infinite energy field that is eternal. You are something that exists beyond the space/time continuum. You have and always will exist in some shape or form.

When I started researching more into this from studying people who had near death experiences (over 10,000 documented now), talking with mediums, my true self, spirit guides, past loved ones, pets, etc., I have learned the message is very similar just with their own touch to it.

All of these things that I talk about in the past paragraph, have been an accumulation of over 8 years and what the core message is, this is not your last life. Life on the other side is much more brilliant than this one. The grand prize is death. Death is birth in disguise. When you were born, you had "died" spiritually in a sense to experience this place called, "Earth." At that exact moment, you were born into the physical world. The same will happen when you return back home. The moment you die, is the moment you are born again. This has been told for eons and there are traditions from specific tribes that do not cry when someone dies. They actually have a celebration because they know, they went back home. They know, they are living in pure bliss, peace and happiness. Why be sad?

This is one of my biggest reasons why I do not like to attend wakes and funerals. I know that these things exist for the sake of the living. But for me, and I have told my family this, when I die, instead of crying tears of sadness, cry tears of joy, happiness and bliss. Focus on the blessings we had in this lifetime to experience in the human form. Know that, regardless what happens, I am closer to you now than I ever have been because when you go back into the spiritual world, there is no time/space continuum. Everything exists only in the NOW.

When you think of your past loved ones, they are instantaneously there. Why do you have to attend a grave where all that remains is the meat suit they used to experience this human life. The real aspects of them are always with you. When you want to communicate, just think of them and instantaneously they are there. I cannot tell you how true this is.

One of the things I noticed growing up was, I can sense and feel energy. We all have this ability. It doesn't make me special. The only difference for me was, I was able to pick up and sense things very easily. My hands and my eyes are what guide me. As I learned more about this later in my life, I started to realize what I could sense. You see, when I was a kid, I could walk into a banquet hall for a party and each table I would walk back, my mood would shift. When I was younger, I could look at people's eyes and see what mood they were in and if, what they were expressing was true or not. It was as if, I had this lie detector within me. Again, we all have this, some more than others.

Long story short, when my grandfather passed away, when I arrived at the nursing home and seeing his body there lifeless, I kept getting this huge nudge and feeling within telling me, I am right here, just not where you see me. And as I kept focusing on his physical body, I felt the warmth and toughness of something on my right shoulder. The feeling is not a sense like me touching your hand, it's different. And I just felt him over my shoulder, kind of hanging out.

The weird thing for me at this time was, I didn't cry much about it. I kept feeling his presence around me and knew that, his physical life is gone but I kept seeing him happy and blissful. Then, during the funeral, it was at the moment of receiving communion, the song, "Con Te Partiro," by Andrea Bocelli and Sarah Brightman was playing. I felt an urge to look up at the altar, where the priest would sit and I saw him walking up the stairs. In this church, the stairs are behind the altar and are on both sides to where they meet at the middle where the tabernacle is located.

I saw him smiling, and as he kept walking up the stairs and got to the top, he did a wave, blew a kiss and it was like a blink of a light and poof, gone. And from that moment, I burst out in tears that I could not control. It was coming out and I just kept my head down because I knew, at that moment, he crossed over.   It took a couple minutes before I could get things back together.

As I reflected on that for 4-6 months before I was going to communicate with a medium to ask so many of the questions I had, I kept seeing the whole thing play out in my head. Even as I am writing this, it continues to play out in my head. When I finally communicated to a medium and asked where he was when he passed (his spirit body), he said it was over my right shoulder. I asked, "When did you cross over into the spiritual world." He said, "On the third day." The third day was the funeral. I asked if he walked up to the top of the altar and he responded, "I went to the top, gave a wave and crossed over at that moment." And as I continued to chat, I understood why all the things ended up the way they did.

One of the things that we talked about is, you choose the experience. You are always choosing the experience and it will never change. It is the blessing of what God gave us when we were created called, "Free Will." And with that, you also get to choose when you are going to crossover.

When I had asked my grandfather, "Why did you pass away when no one was around? No one was there with you?" He said, "Who likes to take a s#%t in front of people?" My grandfather was a direct type of guy. It made sense.

This is not the only time I have felt a soul in a room when they passed. I had a dog named, "Marcelo." He was a Puggle (half pug/half beagle). He was a dog which I loved and appreciated. We had a deep soul connection, and when I needed him at the most times of my life, he would always be there, right by my side and stays there until I moved.

Long story short, when the time comes for all life in the physical form, the end. When Marcelo became paralyzed from the waist down and started to have a severe breathing issue, we were told he wouldn't walk ever again. We had been working with the holistic route for 2 months and slowly got better and then slowly started to decline. Basically, we had to empty his bladder a few times a day since he lost control of his bladder muscles and had to increase abdominal pressure to get him to poop since all muscles at the end were paralyzed.

When we made the choice to put him to sleep, I reached out to a medium I have used many times before, Kate Sitka. She is an amazing medium and definitely gets insights that help you realize the person you are connecting with truly is them.
When I asked her, "What does Marcelo want at this time?" She stated, "He was tired and all he wanted to do is play and run with

his friend." We didn't get the name of the friend, but what came up was a brown dog that had been around us for a while (my wife and I). Just to be clear, we only had Marcelo and then our second dog, Hank, at this time. I never had a dark brown dog in my life.

We asked her more and more questions, to which she was giving us all the information and then she said to my wife and I, "Marcelo is getting restless. He needs you guys right now at this moment." Within 5 seconds, someone came outside and told us, "Marcelo is getting very restless and is looking for you guys."

The hardest choice I ever had to make in my life was putting my dog, Marcelo, down. I will never forget that night nor forget what he taught me that night. Our medium, Kate, told me Marcelo wanted to cross over in my arms. He wanted to cross while I held him. I am a very big softy on the inside, and when she said that, I broke out into tears.

When the moment came and the doctor was explaining what was going to happen and how the process would go. If you never had a dog put down, basically they give the dog a sedative to become calm and relaxed and then initiate the process to pass on.

Marcelo couldn't lie down due to the breathing issue he had. He was fatiguing out of sitting up for almost 12 hours. I would hold him and carry him as much as I could to help give him a break from this.

When the doctor gave the sedative, he immediately lay on his side and I caught him into my arms. I had so much emotions blowing up within me, tons of tears coming out of me, I couldn't look him in the eyes during this process. I kept looking up with my eyes closed and praying for him.

My wife on the other side of the table was watching this and she said, "He kept looking into your eyes until he passed." And it is a moment in my life I won't ever forget. What animals give to us words can never express. But that was not the life transforming moment for me. What happened next, I am going to do my best to share in words.

When I had my eyes closed, and his body became dead weight, I felt something go through my lower abdominal area and come through my body and out the bottom of my neck. It was the weirdest feeling I had ever experienced. I remember telling my wife that night as we took a 1.5 hour walk at 12am to help support one another with our other dog, Hank. I remember telling her, "Marcelo has always been a son of a gun and I know he did that for a reason. What that reason was, I have no clue but I cannot wait to find out."

Long story short, 6 months later, I connected with my medium, Kate, and we had such a great connection for that hour. What she was telling us was unreal. One of my first questions was, "Did we make the right decision? Were you happy with that decision?" Marcelo stated yes but went on to explain how he was tired of this life and how the 2 months of living was something he was trying to do for us, not him and he became exhausted with that."

When I asked him the question about what I thought happened and then asked why, he said, "What you felt was me. It was the part of me that is everlasting. I did this to show you and prove to you that, life goes on. We are eternal, and that; I will always be with you, at all times."

You could imagine the relief and peace I had after that.

Now, I shared all of this with you for one primary reason: This is a dream and the dream is real. But the truth is even richer, fuller and more magnificent.

My grandfather, when I asked what he likes to do most times in the afterlife, he said, "I spend most of my time by the coast, looking at the ocean, drinking my cup of homemade wine. The beautiful part of this side is, I can drink as much wine as I want and I never get drunk or deal with anything afterwards." Marcelo said, "He is playing with his friends, being the young dog that he is and just going to hang out 'there' until my time is up on Earth to reunite. Until then, enjoy your life and know, life continues after this."

I have had other experiences in my life to understand, feel, and appreciate the afterlife. I had a thirst to understand it and spent 3 years researching, reading books, online, videos, etc., to understand it more. I have done different spiritual rituals from different cultures to understand the barriers of the mind and what is on the other side. I did all of this because I knew, if I couldn't get past the fear of death, I would never experience life. I would never truly live. I would only exist. And for some reason, this program of the fear of death was a heavy one. May it be the human collective consciousness, the Catholic church, my family, etc. I needed to know in some shape or form, what that was. And the more I focused, well, you guessed it, the more resources came to give me the information I seeked.

The truth is, you are timeless. The mind can only comprehend 0.0000000000001% of all that is out there. Think about it. All the different perceptions, ideas, knowledge, wisdom, lives, experiences, etc. The mind can only handle that much of it. Your mind is processing millions of millions of bits of information per day, but your mind can only focus on 30-40 of them give or take. Isn't that crazy? The 30-40 is what we focus on and experience. So, when it comes to the full spectrum of what IS, well... Let us just say, what we experience is so limited in this physical world, but it is this limited experience we seek as a spiritual being that is so thrilling.

Let us start by explaining how your FREE WILL works and how you choose any and all experiences in your life. It is not saying, you cannot change it along the way. Most of the time you can. It is like a coach who goes into a game with a specific game plan and if it doesn't work out, he modifies it.

Before you were born, back home in our spiritual realms, you sought out this life, at this specific time to experience something to help your soul expand and evolve. It is not like you just say, I want this and boom. The thing is, there is a lot of planning-out when it comes to creating a physical life. Who are going to be the members of your soul family, joining you on this journey? Who are the ones who will sit on the sidelines in Heaven, to help from there? Who are the people you will interact with and spend time with to help you achieve your goals and experiences? The cool thing about the Universe is, when you are choosing what you want to experience and have in this life, there is always someone there who wants the experience of it also. The Law of Attraction is what I call, "The Fabric Law of Our Universe."

You pick spirit guides, guardian angels and much more who will guard you and help you in this lifetime. These souls' main purpose is to make sure you go into this life, choosing what you want to experience and experiencing that. Usually, there is a theme to it.

I know to some of you, this may sound crazy, but keep an open mind about it. My goal is for you to not take this as absolute truth. Instead, I want you to chew on this for a bit, and when you want more, go for more, when you are done, spit it out.

When all this happens, then there is something created called, "The Blueprint." This blueprint is what you do to construct your life. At what day/time will you be born? Who will be your parents? Closest friends? Who are going to be your family that you are born into? Who will you be close with? Who will you marry or have as a life partner? Who will betray you? Etc. This is all planned out to help you along life to gain the experience YOU CHOSE to experience.

You see, you are creating a movie called, "Your Life," and you are choosing the characters of the movie, the theme of the movie, the storylines, the scripts, the producing, emotions, acting, all of that. You are the creator behind all of this.

"We are the actors, writers, creators, producers and directors of our life and can re-write and re-create anything, anytime!"

Carly Alyssa

You are the one who has created the life you are living right now. This is why many people will say, "Trust the Process." Or "The Universe is working FOR you, not AT you." Or, "You are, right where you need to be, right here, right now." And I can ramble off many other quotes that lead up to this concept.

Wherever you are in your life, it can be changed, improved, maximized, enhanced, expanded, shrink, shrivel, dissipate, etc. It is whatever you choose. And the way you have chosen your life in the spiritual world to experience had to come from much focus. The common theme of my book is all about focus because focus is where you take your source energy and create life with it.

When God blessed us with Free Will, it was God saying, "Go out, explore this Universe, grow, expand and create as I have created you." You have the freedom to experience and create anything you want. There are a couple laws that do exist outside of the Laws of Creation. There is a uniform of respect in the spiritual world that you can never interfere with someone's free will. So the law is stated, "You can create as much as you desire without interfering with another's free will."

This aligns with the whole message of the Universe being your genie. Your wish is my command. The Universe is providing what you desire and you have the team in the spiritual realms and physical realms to help guide you to make sure you experience what you desired to experience for your soul's growth, development, expansion and endless evolvement. :)

Have you ever looked back on your life and reflected on some of the things you did and realized you were in control the whole time? You chose for that experience to be a specific way?

I remember, when I was 24-25, I was truly working on myself to see life in a different lens than what I was seeing it in. During a specific seminar that I attended that was 3 days ,12 hours each day, I started to see how I created the experience I had with my dad. I started to realize that, I had the world's best father, but I was so blinded by what I wanted and what I thought it should be (collective consciousness conditioning my mind) I thought it should have been different. I will never forget the phone call, telling my dad, you have been right all along and I was so stubborn and narrow-minded to listen.

I hope my kid does that with me one day. :)

But, what I saw is that, I held my dad in a box. I had focus on the things I wanted to see in him, instead of who he truly was. Many married couples do this. They see the person and put them in a box rather than seeing them for who they are. It disturbs their image, blocks their light and limits them. And then you wonder why you only see that one side or specific aspect to them. It is because you are focusing on it.

I know in my own marriage, my wife will remind me about how I may put her in a box. I am not perfect. I know these things, but life has a different way of playing out for you. And then, when I see her for who she is, everything changes. It is amazing how that process happens.

So, my question to you is, who are you putting in a box? Who are you limiting and not appreciating who they truly are? Remember, we are human beings. We are perfect because of our imperfections.

In this life, what you are truly focusing on is what creates your experience. Since you focus on something, your mind has to show your eyes how this is true. It has to do this all the time. Anytime you shift focus in your mind, your mind will have to get your eyes to focus on this all the time so you can be shown it to be true. But the key thing is, you are the one who can change the focus to tell the mind to tell the eyes to look at things differently.

When I went through this process with my dad, it wasn't my dad that changed. It wasn't like after a phone call, he was completely different. It was me that changed. It was the way I looked at him. It was the way I talked to him and much more. From there, I started to see a difference in our relationship. It didn't happen overnight, but it happened. And now at 34 years old, I can have a conversation on the phone with my dad for 2 minutes. Before, it just used to be straight to business and that is it. But things have changed and the beauty is, from my perspective, I allowed for him to express himself in a different light than what I thought he was.

What are you doing in your life with others by holding them in a specific way? What are you looking at in your life that you are holding within a box?

All of us are constantly judging, labeling and putting things within a box. It is part of the collective consciousness. And remember, the collective consciousness is the thoughts, emotions and vibrational field of humanity on what they focus on most.

The fun part I have learned over the years is the reinforcement on how you are the one who creates all things. You are the one who creates your life. You are God in your own Universe. Each soul is a micro-universe. And within that micro-universe, they are God. Make sense? :)

And the beauty of it all is, when you come into this physical form called, "A human being," you have what is called, "Spiritual Amnesia." You forget the planning stages. You forget the power you contain. You forget who you truly are. You forget all your other human lives that you are living. And it is a centralized thought. A centralized focus of your source energy that creates this life you are living to have a human being experience.

Now, can you experience all things, as a human, within one lifetime? HELL NO! It is impossible and plus, why would you want to go on a crash course for all of that? Let us share an example.

How many colors exist within the visual spectrum? Some people will say there are 6 main colors: red, orange, yellow, green, blue and purple. But then let's take that even deeper and look at the different variants within one color. The different shades that exist. Then we look at the blend of one color with another and compare that color and then all the shades that exist. As you continue on with this experiment, you will come to infinite because after you go through all the millions upon millions of shades of that one color, then blend, then blend, and end up blending all the combinations, it's infinite and continues to grow.

A human life is like this. It is one singular experience. You were born in a specific era, specific time, day, etc. This was all planned.

If you were one day later born or even hours, everything changes. You chose the parents, the culture, the religion or no religion, ethnic background, friends, etc. And this is at one time and one era that you are experiencing of the collective consciousness of that family, village, state, country, continent, world and Universe. This is all happening within your one lifetime experience.

How many other experiences of the human experience can you experience, if you wanted to experience 50% of the full spectrum of being human? How about 30% or 75%?

You start to see the vastness of this. This is why, one life doesn't work. Why would you come here for one experience and that would be it? How could you take in all the experiences of being human, understand human nature and how this planet works and whatnot?

It is impossible. This is why we live multiple lives. Actually, we are living all of our lives right here, right now. This is more like the hologram breaking off a piece of it, which still you exist 100% whole in there as you experience other lives. But when I talk about this, most people kind of get lost because our mind is programmed to the past, present and future. This is why everything happening instantaneously is a hard concept to grab. Even I have trouble with it at times. I am human, you know. :)

Now, the question to ponder about is, "Since we are the creators of our lives, we create, develop, write, produce, etc., our life and all the experiences it has, is there a way to trust the process and know how we do this?" In other words, is there a GPS system of the blueprint we created?

Well, I can tell you for a fact, there is no physical GPS system that exists, but there is a non-physical one that does. The truth is, a life led with the heart will live in-flow and never resist the beauty life has to offer while the one which is led by the mind will have much frustration, anger, feelings of being overwhelmed, anxiety and end up going through life stressed out. Which one do you want to have?

This is such a cliché', but your heart is the gateway to your soul. Your heart is what knows the way. But the heart is something different than what we are talking about. It is absent of emotions. Instead, it is connected to your TRUE self. Your Source Energy. Your God-self. And when you connect with yourself, it is then, and only then, you will have your GPS system of your life online, connected with you to understand, achieve and see the bigger picture of all things that happen in your life. You start to understand how, "The Universe is working FOR you and not AT you."

This connection is connecting to the Navigator of your soul. When you remember how to connect to this and let it guide your life, life becomes effortless. Life becomes smooth. Life becomes amazing. I am not saying bad days don't happen anymore. They will and continue to show up. Life is all about contrast. But what will happen is you will see the bigger picture behind it. This is why I don't say bad day. Instead, I say, "Character building day." And I sometimes modify it to, what a huge character building day for me. This day is definitely breaking down some old barriers and thought processes.

But when you start to be led by your navigator, you start to understand and trust the process. You start to dance with life and all that life has to throw at you.

"When life throws lemons at you, make lemonade."
Elbert Hubbard

You understand there are things happening at a deeper level and that, your TRUE self would never, ever create or do something you didn't want to. This is a team working for the greater good here. Why would it want to go against what you chose? It cannot for it is YOU.

Imagine life not having any ups or downs, how much fun would this human life be? The human experience is all about the contrast. It is about the ups and the downs. It is what shapes us, guides us, into the direction we stated from day one to experience. I have always said, "If you don't make a change in life, LIFE will make it for you." What I meant about this quote is that, if you are off-track from what you chose to do in this lifetime, LIFE will throw curveballs in every way possible to get you back on your track for you to experience what you came here to experience. This is why it is so essential to learn to connect with your soul's navigator and allow for you to trust the process for that the Universe is always working out for your greatest good and the greatest good of all.

If you miss the message, there will be many more. And if you continue to miss the messages, you will have harder and harder circumstances be thrown at you to get you away from the path you are going and help you onto the path you were destined to be. So, it is very crucial that you connect with Self. Many people in this world are so into selfies, but they don't take enough time to focus on Self. And don't get me wrong, I love me a selfie every once and a while also!

I want to share a story with you that sums up how, when you allow for the flow to happen and know that, life will always guide you to where you need to be. You just need to keep an open mind and trust and know that the Universe is always WORKING FOR YOU.

When I was 19 years old, I was playing rugby at Arizona State University. It was their club team and we would travel around playing D1 schools. The guys I met and the camaraderie of these men was something that still stays present to me. Meeting guys from around the world who were down to earth and just amazing individuals. They loved life and taught me to not be so serious. These men are individuals who I have never forgotten and never will. I only played one year with them, but it was the best year I have ever experienced in playing a sport. So, if you are one of the guys reading this, THANK YOU from the bottom of my heart.

As I played, I started to get into really great condition. I remember after 4-5 months of playing rugby, I was able to run 5-minute miles. It was a feat I always wanted to achieve but never thought it was possible. But, I never gave up on it and I achieved that. As I had such a great physical workout activity to where I would attend rugby practice on Tuesdays and Thursdays at 6pm and finish around 8-8:30pm at night, these practices were never easy at all, even when I got used to all the running and conditioning.

On top of my exercise, I would consume healthy food for the most part. I mean, let's face it, I was in college. Ramen noodles, was my go-to food as I didn't have an oven/stove to cook with at the dorm and all I had was a microwave. Definitely wasn't my proudest moments of eating healthy, but I had to do what I needed to do to survive.

As I started to enter my first 2 months of college, I began to notice how I was starting to become congested all the time. I started to notice, after a couple weeks here and there, my symptoms would continue to increase. I started to have headaches, digestive issues, muscle aches, back/neck pain, sensitivity to light, congestion every day, light-headed at times and so much more.

By the time I was a month away from my first year at Arizona State, I was miserable. I started to feel depressed, exhausted, couldn't sleep, didn't like waking up in the mornings, and my overall mood and quality of life was not what I expected of a 19-year-old.. I was able to run 6-minute miles. I was able to lift double my weight and more. I took supplements daily and drank 1.5 to 2 gallons of water a day. I couldn't figure it out why I would continue to see more and more symptoms.

Long story short, I talked with my mom, and after I had to wait over a month to get into the medical doctor's office, 2 days before my appointment, my mother asked me, "Why not go see Dr. Frank?" Dr. Frank was my mother's chiropractor who she had been going to for almost 18 years at that time. I was willing to give it a shot since I went to him for over a year when I was 10-11 years old. He helped me with my bedwetting problems back then.

I was able to get into his office on the next day, and when I went through the entire exam process and everything else, when it came time for my adjustment, he saw me and said, "You would make the perfect chiropractor." I never knew what he saw that made him say that after 9 years of not seeing me. I don't know, even still to this day, but what I do know is, he sent me a message and planted a seed that I eventually nurtured, watered and let grow.

This was the starting point of how I knew life was guiding me to become a chiropractor. Chiropractors will always say, "Chiropractic found me. I didn't seek Chiropractic." At the time, I was planning on going into Computer Science at ASU, and after 3-4 months, I started to see all my symptoms go away and I ended up getting in the best shape of my life to where I dropped down to 8% body fat, was no longer bloated and so much more, it truly changed and the only thing that changed, was adding Chiropractic.

The amazing thing behind it all is, even though I ended up changing my major to business and finished up another half semester before moving back to Chicago, I still wasn't sold on this thing called, "Chiropractic." Even though I was amazed how a specific adjustment performed to my spine, helped with all my ailments, mood, focus, concentration, sleep, attitude, outlook on life and so much more, I still didn't know if it was right for me. My heart told me yes, but my mind thought something else.

As time went on, I cannot tell you the signs that led me and showed me that I was where I needed to be and the profession I chose was the one that was right for me. I will never forget, the people that came into my life, gave me words of advice, guidance and told me I would make a great doc. They already believed in me before I even believed in myself. And it wasn't until I was 22 years old, working at Triton College's Community Education Center on a Wednesday night and had the pivotal conversation with someone who gave me an advice I didn't think would have happened. It was then and at that moment, I knew it was Chiropractic that I needed to do.

You see, I needed multiple signs. Many signs. Not just one or two. I needed to know for sure within my mind before I decided to move forward. Some people would have just had a health issue be resolved through Chiropractic and restoring the body's communication systems via the nervous system and that was it for them. For me, it was not just that. I wanted to make sure it was for me. I wanted to know within every aspect of myself to know, I was making the right decision for me because one of my worries is not being right or doing something wrong. The fear of making a mistake and having regret later.

The advice I received that Wednesday night talked about me and who I was. Or at least what I appeared to be to this person. Her name was Pat and she talked about, if I truly care for others and want to help others, help improve their lives and make a difference in families and individuals, I have the heart to do that. She went on to say, "Regardless of what you choose, you will always choose what you need, but for whatever it is worth, I believe you are destined to help people for I have seen how much you go out of your way, to just help someone here in this office."

After that night, I submitted my applications the next day and made the decision to become a Chiropractor and what was amazing about it, I ended up choosing the school that I attended over a weekend of visiting. I had to submit my paperwork into another school by Monday to be accepted and start school and I felt like I needed to fly out to Dallas and see what this school was all about. Long story short, after that weekend, I made my decision and moved on. Later in life, I realized that, it was that school I needed to be at. The relationships, the connections, the individuals I met, helped shape me beyond I could ever imagine. But what was the best part of it all is I found two individuals I consider my brothers. These two guys mean the world to me and I would do anything for them. It was these two guys, plus a chiropractic degree and education for why I went there. And from there, coming back home was a whole other process of not knowing I would end up back in Chicago. To be honest, I didn't want to practice at home. I wanted to practice out in Italy. I knew a chiropractor who had a couple doctors out in Italy who I connected with and one of them was going to allow for me to be an associate in his office for a couple years so I can get used to the area and whatnot and then, my goal was going to be, opening up my own office.

The same reason why I flew out to Dallas to see the school on a whim (2 days before the weekend) and why I chose to be a Chiropractor is the same reason why I felt like I needed to come back home. I never knew why at that moment, but time revealed its secrets. For one, my grandfather, who I was very close to, ended up passing away a year and a half later. I found my wife in Chicago. She was the person who took my application for the business association I was applying to be a member. Heck, it took 3 years of knowing each other and then one day, we just went out to have a drink, which I thought wasn't a date, but in the end, it was. And I never look back from that moment. Now, I am very lucky to be called, "Her Husband."

I take a look back on my life and I don't have any regrets at all. Every single moment of your life is shaping you to who you want to become. You are the person in the driver's seat. There is no one else driving the car, except you. Everything you choose, the Universe is WORKING FOR YOU. The Universe is putting all the situations, people, events, etc., to help evolve you to the person you desire.

Always know, regardless how bad something may feel or affect you, always know, this is always working out for your best interest. It is the deepest kind of love and appreciation that you could ever experience. There is so much love and appreciation for your existence for that, nothing would be complete without you. Always know the Universe is always working for you to create the experience you choose, regardless if it is positive or negative. These two concepts only exist based upon a perception of what you focus on. There goes that focus thing again. :)

What I want you to do as we end this chapter is, take a moment and look at all the "bad" times you had in your life. Those rough moments that you thought the whole world was going to end, the failures, the upsets, the regrets and so much more. I want you to visualize them and feel the emotions of them. Once you have them in your mind's eye and feel the emotions in your heart, I want you to sit back from afar, like you are watching a movie of yourself going through everything and look at how that was a blessing in your life. I want you to look at how it shaped you, helped you grow and made you the person you are.

For in life, everything is about the contrast. Without bad, good could not exist. Without hot, cold could not exist. Without the triumphs of life, how could you ever know what good, great, amazing is? Without having these things, life would be BLAH and we all know we wouldn't want to be a part of that.

Trust the process of life for it is always working for you. All things will always work themselves out one way or another. Don't let the moment and fear take over your mind. Allow, trust and enjoy the process. All you need to do is keep your focus on the prize and nothing else. Don't let the distractions get to you. Focus on who you need to be, what are the things you need to associate yourself with and know that, you truly are where you need to be and nowhere else.

Chapter 6

We Are Positive and Negative

"We live in a world of duality. Times of pain are what lead to times of growth. There's always a gain to pain if you master your mind to seek the benefit."

Karen Salmansohn

"Failure is the foundation of success and the means by which it is achieved."

Lao Tzu

The Yin-Yang symbol has always intrigued me in my life. I never fully understood it until I was about 21 years old. And when I started to learn Universal Laws, it started to make more sense to me. It fed my inner thirst for wisdom and truth. And what I learned is that, the Yin-Yang symbol for Taoism is the perfect image of the Law of Duality.

The law of duality states that everything is on a continuum and it has complementary opposites within the whole. You cannot know "good" if you don't know "bad." You cannot know what it feels like to be in the "light" unless you know what it is to be within the "darkness." I was taught around 2011 that, you must embrace your darkness fully in order to truly see the light.

The tension that is created by the duality of opposites, the see-saw of life, allows balance to be achieved. This balance may require you to be so much into the light to feel worthy because you have been so long within the darkness of unworthiness. The beautiful thing about the law of duality is, the farther you have gone down on one side, the further up you will need to go to eventually be in balance. The Law of Duality is designed to continually require to enable you to find your balance and thereafter, to keep within balance. It is what keeps you centered at all times.

The law of duality is what creates the contrast of life. In order for us to truly understand good, we must have bad moments in life. If there is an up, there will be a down. If there is a left, there will be a right. The brain is made up of two hemispheres: left brain and right brain. They are opposites of one another. Your left part of your brain controls the opposite: the right side of your body. Your left brain is responsible for analytical thought, logic, language, reasoning, science and math, writing, number skills and right hand control. The right side of your brain controls the left side of your body. But the right brain is known as the "Abstract brain." Your right side of the brain is more in control of things like, but not limited to: art awareness, creativity, imagination, intuition, insight, holistic thought, music awareness, 3-D forms and left hand control.

You can see just from the basics of what the left and right brain do, you can see that they are complete opposites of one another. But, when we look into the entire universe, we can find polarity in everything. Just in the basic charges of an atom, we have a positive (protons) charges and negative (electrons) charges. These are the fundamental aspects that make up our molecular structure in this universe. But, when we look into the emotions of humans, there are two main emotions that exist and everything else stems from these two things. Love and Fear. Love is the pure opposite of fear. They are on opposite spectrums.

The contrast of life will always share with us that, in order to truly appreciate the good, we must have experienced the bad. One of the quotes I love talks about, in order to be old and wise, we must have been young and stupid. The truth is, we learn from our failures and the truth is, our failures are the beginning of our successes. Look at every successful person, and I know success is measured in different ways for each individual, but when we look at them, they are the sum of many failures in order to be where they are.

No one has ever started into something and was amazing at it. Never experience the feelings of failure. One of the greatest things I love about sports that it teaches you is, how your failures will only sharpen the knife more. I could remember many times, making numerous mistakes in baseball, and I stated, I will master this eventually. Hell, it was another 100s of times of mistakes which were little perfections before I got something down.

Take a look at someone who is learning a new instrument. Do they just come out playing amazing? Never! They have to make mistakes, and the more mistakes they make, the more they are creating the opportunity to play amazing. Yes, persistence plays a role here, but the moral point of the story is your mistakes are paving the way for your success. It happens in every area of life because this law exists within the Universe.

As I am writing this book, I have been truly working on my scoliosis that I have. In the year 2017, we had a reduction in curvature by over 80% in just less than 10 months. It was a huge goal of mine to finally find a method that can help me get my spine as straight as it would be able to. For those that don't know what scoliosis is, there are a few different forms but the one I have is basically, if you look at my back under x-ray from the top of my pelvis up to the base of my neck, you would see an S shape.

As we had success with the change and it staying, there has come a negative side to it. Parts of my body, specifically the right hip, IT band and knee are not responding as well. It has caused me excruciating pain to where I haven't been able to work out or walk well. I was barely able to continue practicing in my office with many nights of resting and ice after a day in the office.

But, as the pain continues to be experienced on a daily basis, based upon the laws of duality, there will come a time for something to replace that pain once the body adapts to these changes. The key is continuing to do the work, focusing on the end in mind and knowing it will happen without no distractions or doubt. And, the beautiful thing is, as time continues to go on, I know the pain will subside and what I will be able to do, will be more than I ever have been able to years ago.

Take a look at your life and take a moment at all the moments that you considered to be bad. How did it all pan out in the end? How much growth did you have from those moments? What did they teach you and share with you?

In order to grow, evolve and expand into the reality you desire will only be determined by the depth of the hardship of what you go through. It has been said before that individuals who had a rough or difficult childhood or growing up, usually have the most powerful stories to share. For example, Tyler Perry went from being homeless to becoming a millionaire in 3 years. Some may say it was luck, but the truth is, he took what he didn't want and let that propel him into creating a different reality.

When I first started out my business, I was very deep into debt. People think of a doctor and think they are very wealthy. The truth be told, based upon an article from The Week, doctors are the top second profession that ends up going bankrupt, right behind professional athletes. (Source: https://bit.ly/2Gk538E)

Now, I could understand this 100% because I fit this description. When I first opened up my business, I was $250,000 in school loan debt. I used to joke around and say, "I own a mortgage for a house, I have no idea where it is, no keys to this house, but I get a bill every single month." The other thing was, I had a drive to start my own business. Some people said, "I was stubborn." But to me, I had a vision and I believed deep within my heart to start my own business. I knew that the worst thing would be, adding more debt on my mile high of it but I was determined. Because if it didn't work out, I could have gone for the other option that people were telling me to do and then, I wouldn't have had that feeling of regret later.

Long story short, I had to put all my business equipment and so forth on credit cards to get by. So, $250,000 in debt plus another $20,000 in debt to just get my business started. After a period of time with operating costs and everything else, I was faced with a decision to either go bankrupt personally to give me some breathing room to focus more on the business or close the business down. I chose to keep the business open and it was one of the best decisions I made. Why? Law of duality.

That moment in my life has propelled me and shown me what I don't want to have. It showed me that, I need to create transformation and stick to the vision I made. I didn't come from a family of wealth or have someone to invest in me. So, I focused on investing 100% into me and my dreams. I was not proud of going bankrupt. It took me an entire year before I made that decision, but I know the Universe had better plans for me. As the years have gone on, I can see why those things had to happen in order for me to discover, expand and evolve into the person I desired to be and the rest has been history since. I never forget that moment because it is what helps me propel and continue moving forward. IT also showed me all the poor thinking, self-sabotage, self-doubt and whatnot I had back then that created it.

When you set your mind to your vision, put your source energy with it by using your focus, the Universe sets things in motion and does the work. It will create events, situations and so forth to help you move forward into the directions you desire and the more you trust, and let go of the mind, the easier and quicker it happens.

Another story on how this works is when I was growing up, my father would have me work laying carpet on the weekends and during the summer. One of the things he would always tell me was, "I am going to show you what hard work is so you don't end up doing the same things as me." A very powerful lesson that I will be forever grateful for. I saw the long days, hours, lost weekends of him having to work just to provide for the family on top of his full time job where he would take any overtime he could. My father was a workaholic, but he was determined to provide for his family in any way he could, even if that meant not being there for a lot of things.

I know growing up what effect that had on me and how I was blinded by not seeing the struggle he had to deal with because bills were coming and if he didn't make the money to keep a roof over our heads, where would we go? I remember my mom telling me there were a couple times where they may have to let the house go but thankfully, everything worked out. These moments in my life showed me, I would never want to have that. As I worked with my dad, it did have a positive and that was a very good work ethic. My father taught me to always do my best work, every single time and never cut corners on someone. But due to going through those pain-in-the-butt experiences as a kid, it taught me a very valuable lesson: I will never allow for work to interfere with my family time. This is why I don't work on the weekends. At this moment of writing this book, I do not have kids yet. But, my schedule is already made up so that, when that happens, I don't have to shuffle anything around. I already created the vision and going to work with having that. Because when I do have kids, I am going to want to spend as much time as I can and cherish every moment.

I know my dad looks back at his life and he knew he had to do what he had to do but this is why now, I try as much as I can to return the favor and spend as much quality time as I can with him. I will be forever grateful for having him in my life.

So this spectrum of opposites truly gives you a gauge to understand that, wherever you are in your life, always know there is another opposite moment coming your way. You just have to do the work during those times, have faith it will all work out (As it always does) and keep your focus on your vision.

The down moments or bad moments that people characterize are really just the Universe challenging your focus and helping you become more focus. You see, if you want to be a millionaire and you are focused on becoming a millionaire but you continue to see bills in the mail, what is the Universe telling you? SHIFT YOUR FOCUS. The results of your life are the living proof of what you are focusing on. Don't let the sheer small moments of downfall, put you away and shift your focus on what it is you desire.

This is why I teach many people, forget the goals, set the vision. What is the vision that you desire? What do you see happening? From that moment, what is it you need to do in order to keep your focus on that vision? How can you ride the waves of life (law of duality) in order to propel you towards that vision?

If we take a look at the most spiritual individuals in the world that have walked this planet, you will find a life of hardship. A life that was of tribulations. It was not a glorious world that they came from. Most of them came from a hard life. One individual who I believe is an amazing soul and I know she is resting in peace is Louise Hays. I loved the concept of what she created and how she created a platform to help transform the consciousness of humanity to higher levels. But, when you look at all the success she created, some say, lucky for her. But was it? Louise grew up in a household that has a violent and abusive stepfather. When she was 5 years old, she was raped by a neighbor. As she went through many ups and downs of life, it wasn't until 1977-78 to where she was diagnosed with an incurable cervical cancer that she realized all was coming from the resentment of her childhood abuse and rape. She had ended up refusing conventional medical treatment and started to go into forgiveness, coupled with therapy, nutrition, reflexology and occasional colonic enemas. The beautiful part of this was, she ended up outliving every doctor who stated she wouldn't live with this incurable cancer.

From that moment on, her life was transformed and she helped transform the world. Her darkest moments help transcend her into amazing moments of life. But the key was, she was not going to let that affect her. She was not going to let that be her ending life story. She focused on something different and then, wanted to share her experience with the world. Since then, she has created a platform to have amazing minds help raise the bar on consciousness and pave a way of life that has been amazing. Hay House Publications has helped me during my dark hours. It helped give me clarity and a way to transform my life, my mind and my thinking. Without it, I don't think I would be here nor be writing this book.

So, know that wherever you are in your life, there is a polar opposite that exists. When you see the stock market drop, don't panic. There will be another moment when it is hitting all-time highs again. It is the law of the Universe. Sometimes, these things happen within a day, a week, a month, a year or even a couple years, but the thing is, eventually, it will return back.

The only time you don't experience the up and down is because you allowed for the down to hold you down. You allowed the down to keep you there and for that, you are so focused on the down, it's hard to realize the ups. It is hard to realize the change. In life, there are so many opportunities for the up after the down. It is like any storm that exists, the sun comes out eventually. The sun will come out but if you keep your head looking down at the mess the storm created, you may miss it.

The beautiful power you have is, with the flip of a switch with your focus, you can transform your path back towards where you desire for it to go. When you start to understand that the ups and downs are seasons and that, eventually, if you are in the valley of the mountains, just keep focus on your vision and eventually, at some moment in time, you will start to trend back up to the peak of the mountains. And if you are in the valley of the mountains right now, you can't see the vision. The mountains are blocking it. But this is when you have to trust the process and know for a fact within that you will achieve this vision and know that, right now I am down, but if I keep moving forward, eventually I will be up. And when you get there, the vision becomes easier to see for nothing blocks your view when you are on top of the mountain.

Realize that and trust that the Universe will always guide you towards the light. But, in order to truly appreciate the light, you have to embrace the darkness. Some spiritual texts will call it the, "shadow of the soul." But to keep this easy, the darkness is any difficult emotion and/or pain. It is the things that you shed away from. It is the things most humans try to avoid.

Human beings would rather pay twice the amount to avoid the pain than just do the work to experience what it is they desire. I was talking to a relationship expert and they were telling me that men dislike rejection, and with her services and one of her programs, men would end up paying twice the amount to avoid the rejection rather than going through the process and learning more about themselves in the mix of it all.

Rejection to me is a part of life. I have experienced it in all facets. I don't like it at all but I am blessed when it comes up. Why? Because it teaches me to keep moving forward. It teaches me to grow. When I work with a patient and they decline care, I will look at that and say to myself, "What did I miss? What communication did I miss? And I will go through the entire process looking for the things I didn't do well or could have communicated better with." Usually, it is the questions to ask to help dive deeper into things. But like anything else, it is a learning process and I am grateful for it.

And through all those rejections I experienced, I have learned how to be better at communicating to patients. Asking the deeper questions and truly being able to share and show the story of what Chiropractic can do to improve their overall quality of life for the rest of their life. I always focus on, when it comes to Chiropractic, how it will make the last years of your life, the best years of your life? When you are being at your best every single day or most days, how important is that to your family? How important is that to your business/career? How important is that to your social life?

I want you to take time here and look at a moment in your life that was a turning point, a moment that shifted you towards the light? What was it? How did it affect you? How much of the darkness were you in? What did you realize when you went through the muddy water to get to the other side? How much happier and lighter did you feel when you did the work?

In the last chapter, I briefly talked about my fear of death. Well, I want to share more of the story here as it applies to the law of duality. In 2013, I was having visions of me leaving this world. They would happen most of the time at night and I could feel me, my soul, leaving as I would feel lighter. And then I get scared and boom, I would be back in my body. For some of you reading this, this may sound weird, but for me, I knew what it felt like to be out of my body from lots of practice of meditation, lucid dreaming and things of those nature.

This scary part started to push me towards facing a deep fear that I had within. And as I started to research and look for sources that talked about death, I wanted to only focus on the lighter side of it (no pun intended). As I went on, I started to hear about something called, "DMT." DMT is N,N-Dimethyltryptamine and this is known as, "The Spirit Molecule." There is a documentary called, "The Spirit Molecule." And when I came across this, I started researching DMT in its fullest. I have heard of it when I was in school learning about different chemicals of the brain and how we have this chemical that is released when we are sleeping that gives us dreams, vivid images and so much more.

As I started down this journey, I wanted to know who has utilized this in the past for spiritual awareness, consciousness expansion and so forth. As I continued to do research, hidden messages along the way came. Long story short, I found out about a brew that has been used for thousands of years in South America (specifically Peru) called, "Ayahuasca." As I have done my research on this, I have found out it is the brew to help guide you within this lifetime. It will show you your deepest fears and help you transcend them. There is much more to this than just that, but it was the basis of what I was looking for.

As I kept doing my research, Ayahuasca kept popping up like the Universe was telling me, this is something you should do. And I even had the resources fall on my lap to where it was a month away and someone shared it with me and I was like, done deal. My girlfriend at the time (now wife), I asked if she would be interested and she was. I told her I had no clue what this would do but all the research and individuals who I looked up that have done it, say it is a blissful experience and one which you truly experience and expand your consciousness.

I will not go into all the details of what I had experienced but I will share my first night. Since I have never used a teacher plant before, this was foreign to me. Letting my body go and not have control is something I am not used to. But, Ayahuasca, the teacher plant, had other ideas for me.

When the ceremony began, and I took my first taste of the brew, which is not pleasant, I went back to lie down and just feel what was going to happen. It was about 45 minutes into the ceremony and I was feeling cold, weak and had that feeling of me, leaving my body again like I was before. All this fear was coming up and I didn't know how to handle it. I kept fighting it and fighting it which only made it worse. Then, when I was an hour into the ceremony, there was another offering to have some more of the brew if you wanted to go deeper. My mindset was like, I am going as deep as I can so I had another, and within 15 minutes, my mind was not allowing me to stay in this reality. It was a battle that I was slowly losing and I have a very stubborn mind, but this one, I knew I was not going to win. The fear of death and all that it was, was right at my door. I remember lying on my side, barely able to angle myself up.

I started to get the feelings that this is what death is. It is a letting go process. It is a process very similar to sleep. You see, when you go to sleep, you don't try sleeping. Sleeping just happens. You don't turn a switch on or off, the body will and knows when to. The same thing was for death. Death is something that just happens. But as I continue on about my story.

What happened next were feelings of like sleeping for 5-10 minutes and then, BOOM! I started to experience the light. I started to feel what bliss was like. I started to feel love, peace and comfort. I started to expand my consciousness and see and feel things that were unreal. It was like I was watching through my mind's eye and had someone guiding me explaining things to me. I know to many, this will sound weird, but when you understand what the teacher plants do, they teach and show you things.

It was showing me how much the fear really is not worth it. It was showing me the bliss of who I am and the power I have within. It was showing me where my source comes from. The energy of who I am. I felt expansive. I was told to enjoy the process. I was like a little kid just being born into this world with AW and excitement. I started to experience the timelessness of who we are. I started to see how this journey in life is just one journey of infinite journeys and that I will always have an existence for we all have an eternal flame that never goes out.

After the first night of the ceremony was over, I felt an overwhelming peace over me. My girlfriend at the time (now wife), looked at me afterwards and said, "your heart is wide open." A friend of ours who was there said, "You look like you are in much peace." I couldn't really talk much because I was overwhelmed in a good way with love, peace and just calmness.

After the weekend, I started to see life different and my mind kicked in and wanted to understand death to the fullest. And this is what gave me a thirst to research for the next 2 years on this topic. I cannot tell you the amount of books, articles, videos, blogs, podcasts, etc., I had listened to because my mind was used to the old thinking and the old fear, but my experience was different and I wanted to figure out how to mend the two together.

It literally took 2 years to where I can honestly say, I feel within who we really are and know that death is only but a disguise for new birth. It is the polar opposite just like in anything else.

Death is seen as this dark, scary event that happens to where you go into a void or nothingness or become nothingness. Some people even believe there is nothing else but this life and once it's over, you are gone forever. But these statements are so far from the truth. The truth is, just like anything else in life, is a huge switch. Death is only but the disguise of a new life. Death is a portal to transfer yourself into a new life, a new beginning. The bliss on the other side is something that will bring tears to you. The love and peace is something that will be mind-blowing for you. And don't worry, you are more complete after death than before death. I will dive more into this in Chapter 10.

During my experience, I had to walk into the darkness in order to truly appreciate my light. I had to dive deep into the darkness as far as I was comfortable doing, in order to truly appreciate and realize the power of my light. It took another two years to truly grasp this experience and all the teachings of what I had learned.

I am not saying I recommend people to do Ayahuasca. What I am recommending is that, trust the process and know that, if you want more love, more bliss, more happiness, you must do the work and dive into the opposite of that. If that means, opening up pain that you buried within your heart because you did not want to deal with it, let it free. If that means you must forgive someone for doing something to you, let it go. The process won't be fun but at the end of the day, the light and bliss that will come from that, is immeasurable. The farther you go into the darkness, the higher you will experience the light. All the greats that have ever walked this planet talk about this in some shape or form.

> "A sensible man will remember that the eyes may be confused in two ways - by a change from light to darkness or from darkness to light; and he will recognize that the same thing happens to the soul."
>
> *Plato*

> "The grave is but a covered bridge Leading from light to light, through a brief darkness!"
>
> *Henry Wadsworth Longfellow*

> "In order for the light to shine so brightly, the darkness must be present."
>
> *Francis Bacon*

> "Desolation is a file, and the endurance of darkness is preparation for great light."
>
> *St. John of the Cross*

> "I will love the light for it shows me the way. Yet I will endure the darkness for it shows me the stars."
>
> *Og Mandino*

The truth will always lie within the pudding. So understand that, when you face difficult times in your life which you will. When you make a mistake, as you will. When you fall short of a goal, which you will. Know that, even though it may feel like a dark time in life, know that, the power of a candle light can only be shown in the mist of the darkness. No one is perfect in this life and no one ever has been. The beautiful thing about being human is, we are faulty. We are not perfection, but the truth is, our imperfections are what make us perfect. And it is through these imperfections that make it perfect for us to discover, expand and evolve.

As we end in this chapter, I wanted to give you a great visual on all of this. You cannot appreciate a sunny day unless you had some cloudy days. You cannot appreciate love, unless you have experienced fear. You cannot experience happiness, unless you experienced sadness. You cannot experience wealth, unless you experienced lack of wealth. You cannot experience true health, unless you truly have experienced a lack of health.

The key point out of all of this is that no matter what you are experiencing, the length in time of how much you will be experiencing that, is up to you. It is until you are sick and tired of whatever that experience is and then, that is when your focus will shift and that is when you will create a more fulfilled and inspired life.

Chapter 7

Biggest Interference Of Life

"The more clearly we can focus our attention on the wonders and realities of the universe about us, the less taste we shall have for destruction."

Rachel Carson

In this chapter, we are going to talk about the one thing that gets in the way of all your successes, dreams and chosen realities. This is the one thing that we constantly interrupt and block the flow towards us. This is called, "The Law of Least Resistance." Many of us do the opposite and choose the path of most resistance. We do this by believing we have to do everything. We have to map everything out. I have to do action steps 1, 2, 3, 4, 5, 6… in order to be successful and so forth. Our minds map out the way the path of success is supposed to look like and if it doesn't follow that path, we get frustrated, upset, angry and much more.

This is a path I have taken so many times. Endlessly having to think things out. In order to create a business, I have to do X, Y, Z, and then this is how it will happen. But, the question is, what if the Universe has a better plan for you?

Have you ever heard the quote:

"Man makes plans … and God laughs."

Michael Chabon

Well, it's true. When we set out to create our plans of how things will be or should be, the Universe laughs. Why? It is humorous for the Universe to have the physical human being believe it sees all perceptions that will guide you towards your greatest goal. Your chosen reality. The Universe has the plan that works best for you and all other human beings that exist.

So, is it worth planning? I still do it but I do it in a way that focuses more on the vision of what I want to do. When I declared I would be the leader in my community when it came to family wellness and make my community the healthiest in the world, I will tell you, outside of giving my practice members the best care I possibly can give, I don't know how the hell that will happen. But, what I have learned along the road has shaped and shifted me towards a plan that is allowing me to take center stage and the funny thing is, it is completely opposite to what I was told to do, what I thought was best and much more. Why do you think that?

The Universe knows what is best for me. It knows, when I set the vision of what I want to accomplish, it will give me that and much more. And sometimes, you ask for an apple and the Universe gives you an orange. It may have not been your choice that you desired but guess what? It's still fruit.

The thing about ourselves is we are always fighting against the flow. As Abraham Hicks shares endlessly about being in the flow or on the path towards least resistance, their work shares endlessly how humans will block the exact thing they desire.

As I have said many times before, "You are your own worst enemy. The biggest battle you will endlessly face is the battle between you and you. There is no other important battle in the world except that one and if you master this battle, you mastered your life."

The collective consciousness of humanity has been shared over years and accepted that, in order to make it in life, you must work hard. You must outwork others. You must hustle and grind. These are terms I constantly hear from speakers that I have gone to see which names I will not mention. The key here is, when I started to realize these words were focusing me on doing the hard work to be successful, I started to get burnt out. There were times I was overwhelmed with things. There were times I was just tired and wanted a break. Ever been there before?

We all have. But then I started to ask the deeper questions, "Am I interfering with the flow? Am I on the path towards most resistance? How can I shift towards the path of least resistance? How do I let go and trust?"

As I kept asking myself these questions during multiple meditations, answers would eventually come. These answers are not what you hear with your ears. These answers are the inner voice, your True voice. It is the one that many people have said God spoke to me. Many people have said, "Jesus told me." Mohammed... Krishna... Shakti... The labels don't matter. But I have always heard this term. For me, it was me. It was the True me. The me that will rejoin back to once this life is over. It was my True self guiding me. And from this perspective, I started to realize this voice more and more and started to show me things, I now laugh at myself and still catch myself from time to time.

I never realized how much I would get in the way of my success. The things I would say, do and move forward. My left brain would get highly logical and when things were low, in the valley of the mountains, I would think I needed to develop a plan. I needed to create new ideas. I needed to do something as quick as I could to get out of this. But, since you read the last chapter, you know, the more I dive deep into the valley, the higher up into the mountains I will be. Instead of trying to figure out what it will be that will help me get to the top of the mountains, how about just BE? How about just accept where you are? There is a reason why you are there.

One thing I have learned in my 34 years on this planet is, everything in this world happens for a reason. It follows closely to the law of focus. Because once you lose focus on something, it doesn't exist anymore (overtime). The same thing is true for things happening for a reason. For example, if we look back in time at things that don't exist anymore, ever ask why? As humanity evolves and grows, the things that gave us survival, are not much needed as they are today. For most homes, we use a furnace and not a wood stove oven. Now, we can go to grocery stores for food, instead of growing our own. Look at how technology is changing every aspect of our lives. Right now, as I am writing this book, we are seeing many retail stores starting to close up their brick and mortar (store fronts) stores because online is where many people are going to. Online is where the market is moving towards. It is not bad. It is a change of living and don't forget one of the rules of creation: The only thing that is constant is change.

So, when you are looking at the events in your life, why did they happen and so much more, always remember, the Universe knows deeper than you. The Universe knows what it is you are desiring. I know when I look back on my life and see some of those dark moments, I actually become grateful for them. And the biggest reason is because it may have shifted me, propelled me, helped me see things differently or make me aware of the things I wasn't before. At the end, it always, and I mean always, worked out for the best and it always will.

The times become turbulent when we get in the way. It is when we don't allow and don't trust the flow. What is this flow? Let us jump into the river and see what that is all about.

Imagine you want to swim 2 miles away from where you are in a lake. The current is pushing towards the beach in rhythm, kind of like ocean waves. You can do one of two things. The first is, path towards most resistance, which means, you swim and continue to swim regardless if the wave is there or not. The second option is, swim for a bit, let wave come and do its thing and then continue swimming. Which swimmer will go farther and be less stressful?

The one who will go farther and burn the least amount of energy about it will be the second way. Why?

Life is all about moving 2 steps forward and sometimes being pushed back 1, 3, 5, X steps back. But as long as you continually move forward, eventually you will get to your goals. When you have no current going against you, that is when you swim and when the current starts to push, you let go and you continue to do this and eventually you will achieve where you wanted to go.

Some may have said, the first swimmer because they won't lose much ground when the current hits them. I agree with you, but, that swimmer will have to use 2-4 times more energy to not lose ground while the other swimmer is just resting for a second before another big burst of swimming.

Over a period of time, swimmer 2 will achieve his goal before swimmer one.

How in life are you swimming upstream? How are you swimming against the current of life? How do you know if you are?

Take a look at your emotions. Your emotions will always be a guide to letting you know where you are with things. Because when you really look at the word, "E-Motions," what that means is energy in motion. E = energy and motion = movement. If you have anger, frustration, disappointment, resentment, etc., these are indicators that you are swimming upstream. You are in the way of what you are choosing to experience.

Let us dive deeper on this concept so you can have a better understanding of how the emotions play a role as a great indicator of what you are doing. You see, in chapter 2, we talked about the power of focus. Focusing on something is what gives life to it. It allows for you to give your power to something. So the moment you focus on something, you are giving it power and giving it life. Now, from that moment on, you continue to focus and follow other universal laws to lead up to where you are right now. You created a plan because you know, if I focus on what I want to see happen, this is how it should play out. But let us say the Universe knows there is something better for you to do that will give you exactly what you want and more of it in a different way. So the one thing you focus so much energy on and expecting it to go a specific way doesn't. What happens next is a reaction and that reaction is going to be one with emotions.

Your emotions are a reaction from a thought and that thought can only exist from what you focus on. So, to put it in an equation

Focus + Thought = Emotion

You have to be careful of what you are focusing on. If you focus on your vision but say, "Universe will provide the best solution for me," if something doesn't happen, frustration won't be there. It cannot be there. Instead, you will be saying, "There must be a different option. The Universe knows best. I am in the flow." As you continue this process, eventually the path comes and you will know because, you guessed it, your emotions will be different.

Instead of the anger, frustration, disappointment and so forth, your emotions will be more of gratitude, appreciation, joy, bliss and happiness. Why? Because you are not fighting up current. You are trusting the process. You are in flow.

Now, let me be clear here, I am not saying being in flow is always a blissful experience. The law of duality will come and when you are ready to truly appreciate and experience your light, there will be dark moments. They always show up first before you reach the light.

Take a look at an individual who wants to become the best guitar player in the world. How many dark moments will happen for that person before they achieve that great light of theirs? And the key thing to remember, the longer you get in the way, the longer it will take before you experience it.

Let me use an example. I remember in business, we shifted gears and started to focus more on families and children because of a long list of reasons, but the main one was, our generation of today, is predicted to not outlive their parents. For me, that was not acceptable on my watch and I was going to share my message as loud as I could to as many people as possible and the ones who were looking for this type of care, playing at your best through all stages of life, would listen and become part of our tribe.

But when I first started, I was mentored by a couple chiropractors on how to do so. They were very successful and had big impacts in their community. It was at the level of where I wanted to play at. So, as I continued to map out the plan, action steps and much more, I had much excitement of all the endless possibilities and who I would become, how I would become the leader of our community and much more. Well, long story short, the more I focused on sharing information out there, by the means of another person, I started to get burnt out after 4-6 months. And the impact I wanted to make was not happening. Instead, I may have done the opposite. And I remember going into a 45-minute meditation to understand what it was I was doing to block my vision and dreams, I started to only see me. It was so vividly clear; it was like looking in the mirror.

So, I stated, I am going to trust flow. I am going to focus on the vision and leave the rest up to the Universe to bring towards me. I stated as I would to a genie, "I declare my vision and know within, you will bring the vision I choose." I knew within that it would happen. I didn't put any expectations on it. I stated, here are the things I will do on a daily basis and leave the rest up to you.

After the first month, what do you think happened? Not a damn thing! Nothing changed at all but instead of normally having my left brain kick in and say I need to do something different, I sat back, focused that energy on my vision instead of wasting it on worry, fear and anxiousness and just kept the vision in my mind. In the second month, do you think something changed? At this point, the Universe was showing me signs I was on the right path. But, it wasn't until 3-4 months when we started to see the shift. We didn't do any special marketing. We didn't do any type of Facebook Ads or anything that many Chiropractors are bombarded with to expand their business. Not one thing changed except for us to be in the flow.

What we ended up doing was trusting the process, and within a matter of 4-5 months, our office went from seeing 5-8% pediatric practice members, to 30-40% practice members. We grew 5-6 times our pediatric practice without doing anything except, focusing on our vision and trusting the Universe would provide. Eventually as things started to move and flow, new ideas and concepts came along the way. New ideas and methods that may be different than the chiropractors I was following. It was like we created our own recipe to share our message with the masses. We were in flow and needed to trust the process along the way. And when we did, it was amazing on how things changed, but I will be honest, when we are not in flow, it still happens and will always happen because I am a human being, we will see a different result and that is the gauge to know where your focus is at.

So, in order to achieve your dreams, step into the flow. Trust the Universe and know all things will always work out for the best, every single time.

Now, some of you may say, "Well, wait a minute, I want to be a millionaire, or start a business but I live paycheck to paycheck, how is that possible?"

First, take a look at the declaration of your situation and then, look at how you see it already impossible. Let me ask you a question, when you were a kid and wanted something and had no money or income, how did you get it?

Many will say, "My parents would buy it." Even though this is to be true, the key concept behind it is this. When you trust the Universe will provide for you always, somehow, the situation would come.

I remember when I was a kid, I didn't have much of the nice clothes like Nike, and other special brands. For us, it was whatever was the most affordable. Plus, I was growing like a weed so things would be outdated pretty quick. But, I remember as a kid, I would want to have nicer set of clothes. I wanted to experience having Nike sweatpants, shirts, workout gear and much more. Long story short, I had a cousin, who is a bit taller and wider than me, lose a ton of weight. I was the guy he would send his clothes to that wouldn't fit. What kind of clothes do you think he had? You guessed it. And I would get a few bags worth.

Not only was I able to save money, which I enjoy doing, I attracted into my life what it is I desired and was not stressing or getting in the way of it. It actually happened without me even knowing it. It was the first time he shared the clothes he didn't need or wear anymore.

Some may ask, what if I never receive something? What if my desire is to be X, but it never happens? The mere essence of this question is going against the river. It is going against the flow of life. The Universe knows best. When I first went into college, I wanted to be in computer science. I loved computers and was fascinated by them. So, even though I put a ton of energy into majoring in computer science and went to one of top 5 in the United States, my path was derailed by the Universe. In the beginning, I ignored it by the type of classes I was not enjoying like Java programming. I disliked this class so much. So, I started to look at ways I could still pick computers but minimize the programming classes I had to take. Well, after meeting my advisor 5 times to change my major 5 times, it ended up the Universe had a different idea.

As I shared my story in Chapter 7, it shifted my journey, bouncing around like a pinball in a pinball machine game.

I don't come from a family of doctors, lawyers and engineers. I come from a blue collar family so I didn't have someone to pick their brain when it came to becoming a chiropractor. This was all foreign to me and the rest of my family. But, I had this voice, this calling that said, "Go this path and you will live an enriched life as you desire to experience." This happened to me during a meditation and I decided to trust it as I have multiple other times in my life.

Well, the rest was history, and as I am writing this book to you, I am still a practicing Chiropractor who loves what he does. Even more so, my biggest joy is adjusting children. First off, they get the power of what chiropractic does and how it truly helps enhance their lives. They don't need to verbalize it, they know intuitively. Second reason is, I get to act like a kid all day long and not be judged from them about it. Talk about a win-win!

And I never regret making that decision for it shifted and changed my life forever. Into a direction I desired for and saw.

Were there many bumps along the road even after choosing to be a chiropractor? More than you could ever imagine. There were heart breaks, disappointments, poor decisions, mistakes, and all others that come with the journey of life and I eventually, embraced them all. They were all set in stone for me for the greatest good. It was put there by the Universe for me to grow, develop and thrive into the person I desired to be.

The amazing thing about this journey of mine has been the endless bumps in the road that show up. It has been something that is teaching me to trust the process and know all things work out as desired. The key is to keep your focus on the vision and not the distractions life throws at you.
So, there is something I want to promise you. It is something I promise every time I do public speaking, corporate wellness, webinars, etc., and that is, I will promise you will have real life applications to execute X, Y, Z, and if I don't help you execute X, Y, Z or give you an understanding of how to execute X, Y, Z, then we will do the work until it happens.

So my promise to you in this book is to make sure I execute a plan for you to help you in this process so you can have something to work with. Something to move you forward and to start putting into action. If you are looking at your life right now and you're asking yourself, what am I not experiencing to the fullest of my desires, let's chat about it.

Take a moment and look at areas of your life that are going very well. I want you to focus on the areas of life into 7 different areas of your life: mental, physical, spiritual, financial, family, social and career. When you look into these different areas of your life, I want you to grade them, 1 being not good at all to a 5, which means, absolutely rocking and killing it.

Mental	1	2	3	4	5
Physical	1	2	3	4	5
Spiritual	1	2	3	4	5
Career	1	2	3	4	5
Family/Marriage	1	2	3	4	5
Financial	1	2	3	4	5
Social Life	1	2	3	4	5

Take time to do this and be 100% honest with yourself. This test is a test only for you and you. You don't have to share this with anyone in your life.

What you will start to notice is, the things that are closer to a 5, are the things you are not worrying about all the time, getting in the way with. Instead, you are more in flow with those things. The ones that are closer to a 1, those are the things that you are getting in the way of. Those are the ones that you are walking down the path of MOST resistance rather than LEAST resistance.

Now for most people, if things are great in that aspect of your life, you will choose a 4. Most people don't experience a 5 because there is always more room for growth and development. When you are at a 5, it means you are doing all the things that exist and there is no more room for growth.

I remember when I marked my past week a 10 out of 10 and my coach laid it on me. He shared with me what a 10 meant and then I said, well, I really felt like it was a 10. Then he asked, "Could there be another experience that can precede this one?" In other words, is this the best it gets? And I was like, "I hope not." And then, this is now why I mark 9.5 out of 10, when I am grading my past week. :)

So, look at your life in these 7 elements and let's talk about how we can transform them to higher levels of what it is you choose to experience because let us be honest here, you are the creator of this movie. You are the writer of your life. You are the producer of the show. You are the wardrobe artist of this life. You choose it all and yes of all, you are the main actor of this movie.

At the end of the day, you get to choose what to experience. You get to choose what it is you want to experience. So anything less than your optimal is because you are not focusing much on it or focusing more on the distractions of it. When it comes to marriage, there are so many intricate parts to a marriage, but the success of the marriage is when both parties are focused on making it successful. When they look at every situation that comes up as an opportunity for growth. It is not about focusing on the negatives or focusing on a habit or characteristic your partner does that upsets you. Instead, look at them in the light that they are and appreciate who they are. Let the challenges of the marriage be the light of your marriage. For that, the darkness of any marriage, will be their greatest light, as long as they stay focused on it.

So what is the great key to achieving the best version of every aspect of your life? It is very simple. I have talked about the first part which is the vision. What is the vision you want to see in the physical element of your body, your mind, your career, etc.? What is the vision going to look like in each area of your life? This is the first step and a step you can't ever lose sights on. Keep the vision clear in your mind, every single day. For some, they may like to see it visually on a board. Go ahead and make a vision board. But keep the vision clear, crystal clear and always focus on and know you are heading this direction and that vision is yours!

The second thing you want to do is consistent action. It is being consistent that makes it happen. It starts to build the momentum of life to support your vision. It starts to raise the vibration, builds up the energy to attract and achieve what it is you desire to experience. It is doing these things daily in order to move yourself towards what it is you desire. Consistency is the key accessing all aspects of life. Nature is very consistent with life and that is why nature will always survive because of this one feature: consistency.

When you set your vision of what it is you desire to experience, you want to be consistent at looking at your vision, but more importantly, taking the steps necessary and consistently to move you towards that vision.
It is called, "The Law of Consistency." What you do on a consistent basis, is what creates your reality. You see, we talked about how words are the fabric to your reality. Well, the words you use over and over again, are the bricks that are laid each day that is building your reality of what you are experiencing. The more you consistently focus on something, the more it brings and creates your reality and your results. You can see the Law of Consistency exists and influences all other laws and they all work together.

You see, the law of association works with the law of consistency by stating, "The more consistent you spend time with certain people, the more consistent you spend time listening, reading, watching, and thinking, the more this attracts and creates the reality you are in right now." It doesn't happen any other way.

Let us use sports as an example. The more you consistently practice at something, the better you become. The less consistent you practice, the less that version of you shows up. In the world today, we have a way of praising people for their success and who they are. It is all we talk about. How successful someone is, how much money they make, the house they have and so much more. But the thing we don't talk about, is their struggles, their battles. What were the battles they faced to get to where they are? How did they do it? What were the top 3 things they did, believed in, in order to be where they are today? What was their darkness that they faced in order to truly appreciate their light?

What you will find in successful people is, they do the things that most people won't do on a consistent basis and eventually, build up enough momentum and energy to achieve those things. It is through consistency that creates your reality and results.

Right now, you have rituals and habits that are either moving you in the direction of your chosen reality or down a path of a lesser than version of the reality you desire. It is either one or the other. And successful people just do the things they need to do on a consistent basis regardless of how they feel, what circumstances are showing up and so forth.

So here is a blueprint to help you achieve your dreams. This is a blueprint to guide you into living a fulfilled and inspired life. Just to be honest, this is not a guarantee. Remember we discussed the BE, DO, HAVE model. Most people will share with you the DO part and not address the BE. The BE is everything. It is what creates the reality of what you choose and it is the essence of where your power is at. So instead of a list of DOING things, the concept of this blueprint is to help you by doing these things, create a relationship with your TRUE self. It is to heighten your focus so you can focus more on the visions and legacy you want to create rather than living in a survival aspect of life.

The first thing that you can start practicing is daily meditation. When we talk about meditation, it is not spending 1 hour a day meditating and trying to not think and have no thoughts. This is not meditation. Meditation is reconnecting with your Source. It is connecting with your True Self. The Self that is timeless and infinite. It is connecting with God. It is connecting with the Universe. Your True Self is an extension of God and so, when you connect with your True Self, you are, at the same exact time, connecting with God.

Meditation is about keeping your mind focused on your stillness. The calmness of yourself. The peace that exists within you. Meditation is designed to help calm the mind and help you focus more. I truly believe meditation is the one thing we all should be doing, outside Chiropractic care. Just like Meditation, Chiropractic care actually helps you connect to your source energy.

What kind of meditation do you need to do? There are endless types of meditations out there. There are many apps that exist to which you can learn how to meditate. There are endless books out there to help you meditate. I am not here to share all those different ones, but what I can do is guide you to a source.

I meditate 10-30 minutes per day. Some days, I will meditate up to an hour. It just varies on what is needed, the level of peace I am at during my meditation and any insights I may be receiving at that time. Sometimes, I just meditate for an hour to bliss out and enjoy the peace and bliss that comes from it. I know that if I don't meditate in a day, it truly affects me as I didn't connect with my source and the essence of who I really am.

"If every 8 year old in the world is taught meditation, we will eliminate violence from the world within one generation."

Dalai Lama

I wholeheartedly agree with this statement because when you start to create a connection with your True Self, that True Self is LOVE. How could violence exist if you have love in your heart?

When you are filled with it? It is like saying, you can have disease when your body is 100% healthy. It is impossible. The more love you have within, the less the other side of things will exist.

So, the first thing you can do is start with a daily meditation for 10 minutes. The first few handfuls may not be fun. For some, it may be calming in the beginning, but then, that focus will be all on the thoughts flying through your head instead of focusing on the stillness of you. Eventually, you will build this muscle up to where you can instantaneously focus on the stillness and still be aware of all the thoughts flying by but not give energy to them.

When you meditate, it increases your focus by 30% and your productivity for the day by 50%. Who wouldn't want more of that?! Meditation will transform your life only and only if, you practice consistently.

I perform meditation classes in my office and when I am done with the workshop and guided meditation, I always leave them with a challenge and the challenge is, mediate for 30 days straight and when that happens, meditate for another 60 days straight. I tell them, if you want to make meditation part of your life, you need to meditate for 90 days straight. And if you happen to miss one day, you have to reset it. This is how the brain operates and creates patterns and habits. In the first 30 days, this is what it takes to break a habit. In the next 60, it is what it takes to connect and make it a lifestyle. As I am writing this, I took on a challenge and on this day I am writing this book, I have meditated for 219 days straight on top of the other things I will share with you. Meditation is an essential part of my lifestyle, and regardless of the benefits of it, what makes me do it every single day is the connection with me. The connection with who I am. It is priceless and it allows for me to handle my life better, not get distracted and bring more of the real ME into every aspect of my life. I cannot emphasize enough on how meditation is crucial for your growth.

Now, where to get access to the vastness of mediation. Check out YouTube and all the different apps that exist on your phones. One app I was introduced by a practice member in my office called, "Insight Timer," is a cool app to use. Tons of different meditations on there and most of my practice members love it and use it daily. Check them out.

The second thing I do daily that helps center me and get prepared for the day is breath work. I perform many different types of break work, but the main one I utilize is a method called, "Wim Hof Method." The Wim Hof Method is a breath work I have been using for the past few years and it truly has changed my life. Not only does the body need oxygen to live and thrive, but also the stimulus of your vagus nerve, which is a part of the nervous system for calming, relaxing, growth and development; this process definitely works.

Basically, and I recommend checking out WimHofMethod.com for the full details and different variations to his breath work, is basically you breathe in through your mouth as fast as you can and then, just rest your ribs and stomach to let the air out. You would perform this for a specific amount of reps and then on your last breath, you would hold your breath for as long as you can. The longest I ever held my breath for was 4:10 seconds. Crazy I know. But, the key is not about the holding the time for how long the breath is held, it is the peace in-between it that matters. This is where I do my visualizations when I hold my breath. This is when I focus on my visions of what I choose to experience and make it happen.

The third thing to do is appreciation of someone. For me, every day, I will share a video, text message, share it in person, etc., of what I appreciate, honor and/or love about my wife that day. I do this not for the sake of any reason and trust me, when we get in an argument or not connecting that day, I still have to come up with something and dig deep. Again, consistency is key, but when I do these things, it helps me stay focused on the positives, even when I want to stay on the negative side so much, it helps break it down. This is the goal of your focus and not letting the distractions get to you.

Hell, every marriage, you are going to get into fights, say the wrong thing, do the wrong things and so much more. It will endlessly happen, but the key is, through all of that, how do you keep your focus on your vision? How do you not allow for the distractions to pull away from what you really wanted to experience in the marriage? This is the key, and for me, letting my wife know how I feel about her and what I appreciate about her every single day, helps us in our marriage and I never want her to not know how I feel about her in any given day.

Because at the end of the day, we are only here for a short period of time. We are only here for what is a blink of an eye in the spiritual realms. I don't share what I appreciate and honor my wife every day for me. It truly is for her. It is my honor to have her in my life. For her to accept me for all my mishaps, mistakes and imperfections, is an honor to spend her time with me and that is something I will forever be grateful for.

Now, if you don't have a significant other or life partner, who is someone in your life you appreciate? Could it be your parents? A friend? Family member? Teacher? Coach? The thing is, you can share each day with someone different. The key thing is, tapping into appreciation and gratitude. And the more you do this every day, the more you focus on this, the more you will see the light in the darkness. The more you will see the blessings in disguise when the storms come. Why?

Well, without storms, nature does not get a vital nutrient that it needs just as much as we do: water. When the storms come, it cleans the air, gives fresh carbon dioxide to the trees and gives life. Lighting storms help re-energize the earth by striking the water and the ground. As I said, there is always a reason for everything and I truly believe we are just in the beginning of understanding why. That is the beauty of life. It is ever-expanding.

These three things are essential for you to connect to who you are. Meditation, breath work and sharing appreciation. For some, if the sharing appreciation daily is not your thing, then focus on creating a gratitude journal. Something every day of what you are grateful for and put your energy into it. Really tap into what truly you were grateful for. At first, it will be the small things like I am alive, the sun's out, good weather, etc., but eventually, it will become smaller and more specific and that way, you are truly starting to appreciate every fabric of life but more importantly, rewiring the brain to focus more on gratitude and appreciation. And what happens when you shift your focus? You got it! It shifts your life!

The other thing I do is movement. Do some form of movement and/or exercise. This can be going to the gym, yoga, Qi-Gong, Tai-Chi, etc. The key is doing something for a minimum of 10 minutes of movement. This helps energize the body and get the body moving. Actually, the movement stimulates different areas of the brain to wake you up. So, exercise is a great form to utilize first thing to get things moving and truly wake yourself up. And again, it is just 10 minutes to do.

These 4 elements are what help keep your focus on the prize. Help you keep your focus on the Source of your life, YOU. It helps you strengthen your focus so you are less distracted and help you see the bigger picture in things. But the magic is not in the doing but in the BEING while you are doing.

I remember when I used to make it a goal to hammer out all of these for X amount of days in a row and I would. Sometimes, 90 days straight and I wouldn't feel calmer but actually more stressed out. I didn't understand it until a few years later but what I started to figure out was, I was checking the boxes rather than being there in the present, focusing on my energy and showing up. You see, when you just check the boxes, you are doing the work but you are on autopilot. There really is no magic. This magic is your energy that comes from your focus. You see, the more you utilize your focus, the more it becomes alive and the key thing with meditation is to focus on the stillness to create a deeper connection with yourself which results in a deeper connection with all other things.

The more you focus on breath work and actually do the work but being present, the more you can tap into this power source and awaken and feel every single cell in your body be awakened.

The more you show appreciation and gratitude for all things, the more you start to see the bigger picture in things and start to realize the law of duality in all aspects that when you are in the darkness, you are one thought away from experiencing the light.

And lastly, movement is the key. As you keep your energy moving, the more momentum you build up in your life and the more you challenge the body to take things to the next level. The more you stress your body, the more you are allowing it to stay fit and handle stress in a more adaptable and thriving way.

If you practice these 4 things on a daily basis for the next 90 days and truly put your energy into this without checking the boxes, you will discover more of who you really are and from that moment, the things in your life will expand and you will start to evolve into the person you choose to BE. You will start to experience higher levels of every fabric of life because you are setting the stage on a daily basis.

Now, I am not saying bad days will come. I am not saying you won't experience the dark. Hell, those things are endless. But what it will do, is strengthen you and you will see the purpose behind it.

There are many things that have shown up in my business and life in 2017 that radically propelled me to do things differently and even though it was hard and definitely put me far out of my comfort zone, I kept seeing the bigger picture and knew that, I just needed to take a step back, let go and trust the flow. From there, it put a fire under my ass to get this book I wanted to write for a few years done. This book you are reading took me 54 days to write from beginning to end. And that is because I accepted neither more stories nor excuses. If I really wanted to have my book done and out there, I needed to get super focused on it and stop letting distractions get in the way. And, the beautiful part is, it happened and I was getting in the way with the distractions rather than focusing on the prize.

Chapter 8

Language of the Universe

> "We are all cells in the body of humanity. We are not separate from our fellow humans. The whole thing is a totality."
>
> — *Peace Pilgrim*

As in all living things, there is a communication system that exists. What science has shown us is there is even a communication system that exists from the roots of the trees and when there is a drought, the big trees will give water to the little ones. There is fungus in the soil that acts as a huge communication system. Plants and insects work with one another. The smell of grass being cut is actually a communication system happening. Our bodies have a very in-depth communication system called, "The Nervous System." Every single living organism has some form of communication in some shape or another. No organism exists without a communication system.

As nature has one, so does the Universe. The Universe has its own communication system.

> "If you wish to understand the Universe, think of energy, frequency and vibration."
>
> — *Nikola Tesla*

When we put it into this content, there is one word that explains how the Universe truly communicates and this is through "tone" or "tonal." When we look at the definition of Tonal from the Webster Dictionary, it states, "having tonality; employing variations in pitch to distinguish meanings of otherwise similar words.

When we think of what the Universe means, it literally means, "One Verse." One verse in a song. And we, all the souls that play in the big game called, "LIFE," are all a musical note to this One-Verse. But this Universe cannot exist unless it has all of its notes to play its song.

So, when we think of tone, it is very easily understood like the tone of a guitar string. The tone of a piano key, violin, cello, etc. Each aspect of this Universe vibrates in a specific frequency that creates a tone. Science is starting to understand this concept so much more. If you want to see how tone plays a role on images of sand, look up on YouTube - Resonance Experiment with Tones. This is something called, "Cymatics," and in this video, they use salt on a plate to show resonance and the different shapes that will be created based upon the different tone/vibration that you will hear. It truly is amazing.

Throughout this chapter, I will say tone or vibration but they are interchangeable. They mean the exact same thing. The level of tone is determined by vibration. Higher vibration = higher tone. Lower vibration = lower tone. So, the entire universe communicates off different frequencies, vibrations/tones. Each tone has a whole different experience and reality compared to the other. You, the essence of who you are, have your own tone, and based upon the tone that you are vibrating at, manifests your reality.

This is the main emphasis of why many people say, "The entire universe is governed by the Law of Attraction." If you have seen the documentary movie, "The Secret," then you know exactly what I am talking about. If you have not, take a moment and watch it on Netflix, Hulu or rent it. This will give you the framework to understand what I am explaining in this chapter.

In a basic explanation, the Law of Attraction basically means, "Like attracts like." In order for you to experience and manifest anything into your reality, you must be in resonance or same tone as the thing you are choosing to experience. So for example, let us say in order to experience happiness, you need to vibrate at a level of 500 and you are only at 400, you will never experience happiness unless you raise your tone to the level of 500 and then and only then, you open the door to experience happiness.

The tone is what indicates the experience. And you, are the one who chooses the tone you desire to be at. And the consistency of the tone that you choose will help shift your vibrations closer to that reality of what you are choosing to experience. This is why consistency is king/queen. Because if you do not keep consistency towards what you choose to experience, you will never experience it in your reality or it will take a very long time.

The law of vibration works off every single thing. It's what the Universe is responding to at all times, regardless if you believe it or not. Every thought you focus on, every emotion you have, every story you believe in, every belief system you fall under, all of these things fall under this law and what create our reality.

There are more than just this but to keep it simple, these are the three things that raise or lower your vibration. The first as we went in depth during Chapter 2 is what you focus on. Whenever you focus on something, your energy flows towards and gives life to it. For example, I didn't put thought up there because in order for you to have a thought, you need to focus on one of them. The thing is, you have over 50,000 thoughts per day, but your mind will only focus on a percentage less than 0.001% of them. You are the one that has to focus on the thoughts that are flying by.

The second is emotions. As I will share with you in just a few, your emotions are what raise or lower the tone of yourself. Think about a time when you were really excited and happy about something. Was your tone low or was it high? Now, think about a time when you were sad and depressed. Was your tone high or low?

If you really thought about something, you will feel a lightness about you when you think of the thought of something being excited/happy and you will feel a heaviness when you think of something sad or upset. This is the essence of tone and your emotions play a big role in all of this because it is what raises you up or brings you down.

The last part is the words you choose because words are merely vibration. Words are just tone. Words are like notes within a song. And whenever you share a story, it is like playing a song and the notes you are using is what determines the tone of the song that projects to the universe. Then, law of attraction goes to work and brings whatever tone that you have projected outwards.

This is why we have to choose our words wisely. We have to wisely choose where we put our attention/focus to. Because every single day, these things are orchestrating the reality we are experiencing right now. And I know for some, you may be feeling, this is hard work and the truth be told, it is not. All it is, is a way to think differently than before. It is a way to understand the inner workings of your world, your universe and how you can create a more fulfilled and inspired life if you choose so. Because at the end of the day, what you are experiencing in your lifetime is all based upon you and you. There are no victims and the mindset of being a victim is more of an illusion. Things happen to people and sometimes it is not great, but it was meant to be there for a purpose, for a reason. And it is up to you to focus on what part of that event do you want it to mean for you in your life? We talked about this with the Law of Duality. You can let something dark either keep you in the dark, or you can go down to the depths of it, face it and allow your light to shine. Because in this life, the only way to truly appreciate your light is by the amount of darkness you face within.

The one thing I know about this law and all the laws I have shared with you as of now, is they only exist in this Universe. In another Universe, there is a whole new playing field. There is a whole new set of laws that I have no clue what it would be for I am not there to experience it. You see, if you think of each Universe as a sport, you will start to see how this Universe could be like football and the next is soccer, and the next is baseball and so forth. Each Universe is a different playing field with different rules and laws that exist within them. So, until we can inter-universe travel, this will hold true for now. :)

So, how does the process work for law of attraction? How can we change the patterns we have created?

The only way we can truly make change is from within. Your entire world and all that you experience is because of the relationship you have with yourself. Every single thing you experience is all a mirror reflection of you. If you don't have trust in yourself, what are you telling the Universe and your brain? Prove to me that I cannot trust someone or something. And what lineup of events will happen? You will continually to see things happen where someone will betray you, lie, dishonor you, etc. It will continue to happen unless you start to change your story. Until you start to change your thoughts and emotions. Until you start to change your focus, you will continue to experience the same old thing.

The same is true if you have self-doubt. What if you don't have self-love? What if you don't have self-acceptance? What if you don't have self-worth? Each of these things come from what you focus on first, then relates to an emotion and then you choose the words.

Take a moment and look at something in your life that you are not happy with. Something that you would call a weakness or a fear. It can be public speaking, being in big crowds, not big crowds, difficult conversations, etc. What is that one thing you dislike to do?

Now, let us take a moment and look at the focus you have when it comes to that. When you think of that THING, your mind will create a reactiveness of what you constantly focus about this. Then, you will have an emotional response that you have programmed yourself to have about this concept and then, you will express it in words that resonate with the feelings and emotions that relate to it. All of these things vibrate at a specific tone, and when you continue to do this, you are sharing that tone to the

Universe and then you wonder why your only experience is that and the reason being is because you are sharing the tone off into the Universe to respond back to you the reality you are choosing.

This is as simple as choosing a radio station to listen to. The tone/vibration is the station itself. It is the experience once YOU tune into it. Remember in the Laws of Creation by Bashar, #4 states, "What you put out is what you get back." This is how you end up in an endless loop of experiences that are the same.

"Insanity is repeating the same mistakes and expecting different results."

Narcotics Anonymous

How can you expect different results with the same mind? The same focus? The same language? The same emotions towards that event? This is insanity and many of us, including myself, are creating this day in and day out and cannot figure why this happens to me.

For example, imagine you catch yourself complaining about a car you have had for the past 4 years. Every time you get in, you are focused on the things that you dislike, don't like and can't stand. The more you focus on these things, your emotions of disappointment, frustration, aggravation, etc., kick in and the words you choose are as shared above, don't like, dislike, hate, etc. to express yourself. You are driving and you see the car you want and say to yourself, "I would be happier and appreciate having a car like that." You can see yourself in there happy and joyful. Six months later, you decided it was time to buy that new car and you do. For the first 1-2 months, you are all excited and happy. You are showing it off to friends and family. You are loving the new car smell and feeling great. Once all of that wears off and IF you never changed your mind, within 6 months to a year, you will be back at the same place you were with your other car. You will focus on the things it lacks, dislike, not up to your standards and so much more. And you will go down this endless cycle until you realize it all started with you. If you changed your focus, your emotions and your words, you will start to notice things will change. You start to change the radio station to appreciation and gratitude to your car and a whole new experience will come from that.

Again, this plays a role in every fabric of life since it is always working and never takes a break. Another example is in a marriage or relationship. You are focused on the things your partner does not do well or what annoys you. You have an emotional reaction to it and start using words repeatedly about the situation. You start to look at other couples and see how happy and in unison they are with one another and wish you had that. You start to focus on the lack, and as you know by now, what you focus on is what becomes your reality so you start to notice more and more lack in your relationship. You state to yourself, "I want a different experience." So you buy the best book on relationships and do all that they tell you to do. You listen to the best relationship podcasts and follow their advice. You continue to do what is told but you NEVER changed your focus. You never changed your mindset and what you are looking at all the time. The things you focus on work for a short period of time but then, the problems slowly swing back in because you never changed you.

Law of attraction is always showing you what you have within. It is always showing you what you focus on most. It is always showing you what emotions you have attached to specific things that you focus on and then, the words you use to express those things. It is always working to show you what you are sharing with it.
No matter where you are in your life, you can radically change it. It doesn't take hard work. It just takes awareness. It just takes a moment for you to change your focus, change your emotions and change the words you are using. These play a massive role into the experiences you have today.

Another example is the relationship people have with money. As I stated earlier, I grew up with individuals who believed that money attracts money (law of attraction working here), more money = more headaches, more money = less happiness. These are very strong negative belief systems about money. If you have one of these, when you see someone super successful, big house, nice car, etc., what is your first reaction? Your reaction is all based upon your focus. The second is the emotions that come from this. The third then, is the story you tell yourself. If you believe money only goes to money and you are not getting any money, what does that tell you? Your mindset is one of poverty. It means you are not worth it. You don't deserve that. There is some negative belief system built within you and unfortunately, it was not yours to begin with. This was something learned.

How do you break away? First start by changing your focus about money. There are many beliefs about money, pick one you like. For me, money is life's energy. Money is a relationship and that relationship is what I have with money. If I abuse my money, less comes to me. If I don't show appreciation of the money I have, less comes to me. I have to shift my focus first. And one of the biggest things that helped me shift my focus was, based upon 2017, there is over $1.2 quadrillion dollars in all markets, real estate, derivatives and so forth. Quadrillion is a 1 with 15 0s following it. If we divided the world's population by rounding up, that would be $150,000 per person on this planet. There is endless money that exists.

Now, I know some may think, well, mainly the 1% own most of it. The facts are true. 1% does own majority of the riches of the world. But why? Inherited? Maybe. Law of Attraction, yes. How so?

Based upon the law of attraction and tone, everything in your experience is based upon the tone that you are at. And this tone is determined by your focus, your emotions and your words. So, if you gave everyone a million dollars and kept their focus, emotions and tones of what they do on a consistent basis the same, what will happen? Will everyone become richer? Would some become poor again?

Based upon the law of attraction, the people who are wealthy, will end up with majority of the money within 1 year due to the tone they vibrate at. Remember before, money likes money. Law of vibration is all about like attracting like. And so, if you have a strong and balanced money consciousness, a high vibration of money, you will be successful in the things you do on a monetary level.

If you are choosing to tune into the radio station that is making $50,000 a year, regardless of what you do, you will end up at the $50,000 mark every single time.

> **"You cannot have a different experience unless you change the tone of what it is you are relating to."**
>
> *Dr. Victor Manzo Jr.*

If you have $100,000 radio station that you are tuned into, regardless of what you do, you will always be at $100,000 unless you change the station. Why do you think for most people who win the lottery, they end up bankrupt? It all has to do with the radio station they are tuned into. It has to do with the channel they are on. They have a frequency that creates a specific station. I will never forget the experience I had with this.

I learned about this concept sometime in 2012-2013. And I started to change my focus, shift my emotions and be aware of the words I was using. In 2014, I was determined to grow my business to the next level. We just signed a lease for 5 years for 3,000 sqft. At the time, our rent was around 20% of our overhead. I knew in order to play at another level, I had to take a risk and this is what I ended up doing. As I kept my focus on growth, serving more patients and being a resource to the community, changed my emotions that I had with myself and money and focused on new vocabulary to use, we saw a massive shift at the end of that year. The business grew 84% within one year. And I told myself in the new year, I have to change my focus, words and emotions in order to hit new highs and we did. We grew another 48% the next year.

When we look at billionaires and millionaires, they are the same as you. They have the same stuff, same experiences with emotions and they also have the same time in a day. The only reason why things are different all has to come down to the law of attraction. What are you attracting in your life compared to them? And this will all start with your focus, emotions, and words. It is not that billionaires and millionaires work harder than you or are smarter than you. They just focus on things differently than you. They put different emotions to things and choose their words wisely.

For example, when I first started to do public speaking, I would always feel nervous, worried to make a mistake and didn't want to forget sharing something. I would study, practice, read books on presenting, did Toast Masters and much more. The nervousness would overtake me and make it hard for me to enjoy the process of public speaking. I would get jealous on how public speakers make it seem so easy but yet, I cannot appear that way. Until, one day, I changed my focus. And my focus changed everything leading to public speaking to where now, I make a mistake, I will joke about it.

The focus shift for me was, "If I worry about what people will think of me and what mistakes I may make, I am cutting them short on the message I am trying to share and sometimes that can be life or death for some." Once I started to shift my focus on this rather than me, I started to realize the selfishness I had and shifted towards serving and being selfless. And at this point in the game, do I get nervousness anymore? Of course! That never goes away! But it only exists within the first 1-2 minutes max and then, I get into my centered place and have fun inspiring and sharing with others. The same goes for you. If you dislike something or are afraid of something, there is a focus you have. And all you have to do is change your focus, change the emotions tied to it and use different words to make up a new story about it. And from there, let the Law of Attraction go to work and watch you experience something totally different than you ever have before.

One of the ways you can start to attract the life you desire is by affirmations. Affirmations are a declaration of what you state you are or choose to experience. For example, every morning I wake up, I have 5 basic affirmations that I state every day.

- ***I am in a constant state of growth and expansion***
- ***I am powerful beyond measure***
- ***I am abundance***
- ***I am the best communicator and speaker***
- ***I am a powerful manifestor***

Now, I do change my affirmations each year, but this is what I declared for 2018. These are the 5 things I will tell myself every single day. The reason behind this is to declare to the Universe, this is who I am. To declare to the Universe, this is the experience I am choosing to experience. But the words and the statements are not enough to make it a reality and truly get the law of attraction to work for me. I need to add in the second component which is emotions. I need to come from a powerful state. As Tony Robbins calls it, "You must be in state." When he states this, he means a powerful state of mind. It is when you feel overall powerful. You cannot think this. You must feel this. This is the vast difference.

So, when I state these affirmations, I state them with an emotion that makes me feel powerful and certain. One of the things I do is, I will think of a time in my life that I overcame a difficult time. I will think of something when I faced my fears or broke out of an uncomfortable situation to be successful. Most of the time, for me, it is in sports that bring the most memories. And I have many of them, but there are a few when the game was riding on me to get the base hit or I came into a game to close for the win. Or made a diving catch and then threw out a guy at home afterwards which would have given them the lead or tie the game.

When I do this, it helps raise my emotions which raises my tone and allows for me to come from a more powerful state, and the higher the tone/state you are in when you do affirmations, the more magnetic you become to attract these things into your life.

> ## "Every word you speak is an affirmation. The subconscious is always listening."
>
> *Louise Hay*

This is why I have stated throughout this chapter, the third factor is the words you choose. It is what the Universe is constantly listening to. This is why I dedicated a whole chapter to the words you choose. Each word you choose has a tone and that tone will dictate a part of your reality.

So, why is it you can describe words all day long, but if you don't put emotions behind it, it makes it harder to manifest? Remember how we have been talking about tone this whole time. Well, emotions have their own range of tone and vibrations. This is all based upon the work done by Dr. David Hawkins and broken down in his book, "Power vs Force." When we look at each emotion, there is a tone that exists with it. A vibration if you will. Dr. Hawkins doesn't explain it in this way. Instead, the numbers are a level of consciousness. For me and my understanding, I look at it as tone or vibration.

Anything above 200 is a state of expansion and anything under 200 is a state of contracting. When you are utilizing your affirmations, choosing thoughts, picking emotions to experience, you want to evolve and expand towards the higher levels. So, when it comes to creating a bigger attracting power, choose emotions that are higher on the totem pole. The higher the number, the more power you have vs the lower.

For more information to go deeper on this concept, please visit the works of Dr. David Hawkins and Abraham-Hicks as they go much deeper on this concept than I am.

So, the key concept here in this chapter is to analyze your life and be aware of what you are focusing on in different elements of your life. These different elements are going to indicate what you are focusing on, what emotions you feel and the words you use to express them. These are the things that will be attracting the experience you are choosing by doing these three things.

Remember that if you don't like what you are experiencing, change the focus, change the emotions and change the story (the words you use to express it). From there, over time, you will start to experience something different and the Universe will slowly start to show you how you are on track for what you are creating. Always remember, it is always working and always listening. This process is learning an entire new language. It will take time and it will take some new neuroreprogramming to achieve. In my group coaching and online programs, this is a huge concept I work with on how to help you shift and transform over a period of time to achieve these results and have your mind constantly be working for you and not against you.

In the beginning, this process is not simple and it takes some work to achieve because you have been conditioned and programmed yourself in a way to be experiencing where you are right now. We need to work on shifting that perception and the focus to start shifting you towards a new reality of what you desire, and it takes work. It will take a minimum of 30 days to just break down the habits and patterns your brain is experiencing and then another 60 days on top of the 30 (total of 90 days) to retrain the brain and program it to a new perspective. This is basic neuropatterning. Once the brain makes the shift, you now have tuned in, chose a radio station, of what it is you choose to experience.

So, one last way to truly focus on things and to create an attraction is when you focus on being happy at work, don't just think of the word, "happy." I want you to see yourself being happy, walking with a pep in your step and just enjoying the process of work. I want you to see yourself smiling and interacting with people. These are the things that will matter most.

I remember when I wanted to grow my business to new levels; I was focusing on seeing more patients in the office, workshops, and so much more. I was putting my energy and focus on there and what happened in the next 4 months was nothing much. We grew but it wasn't much. Then, I started to shift my focus and start focusing on my vision and focus on myself being happy in the office, connecting with my practice members, serving at 100% and being that resource in their lives to help them find/stay on their Wellness Path. And every day, 1-2 times per day, I would focus only on this. I envisioned my staff being happy and just walking out of the office at the end of the day, accomplished, calm and light.

What do you think happened in the next 4 months? 6 months? The practice shifted and changed. It grew. It started to vibe more. I remember a team member of our office shared with us, "the energy has shifted in this office. IT feels good. I don't know how to explain it." And the truth is, we changed our focus, changed the emotions we were attaching to things and changed the story/

words we used to express it all. Over a period of time, we manifested this by using the Law of attraction that has created an office we all look forward to going to and love being at. It didn't happen overnight. And the next year or two that has followed has been life changing. Each person that is in our office is there for the right reasons. And we focused on attracting the practice members that are looking to maximize their human potential and invest in their health. This is the service we offer and we wanted to make sure each person that walks into our office is looking for that.

I can give you endless experiences of my own on how this works, but the factor comes down to you trusting the process and knowing it works. Knowing it works just like another law, "Law of Gravity." Regardless if you believe in this law or not, it exists. Same with the Law of Attraction. Regardless if you believe in this law or not, it exists. And in order for you to expand your life in the direction you desire to feel more inspired and fulfilled, one must shift focus, emotions and words to experience one's heart's desires.

Chapter 9

Our Minds Contain Limited Information

If you refuse to drink from the fountain of knowledge, you'll die of thirst in the desert of ignorance.

Anonymous

When it comes to learning, growing, adapting and evolving, the word, "I know," is something we can clear out of our vocabulary. For the word in of itself means, "You know all that you need to know about something." It halts growth, learning, expertise and so forth. One of the things I never want to call myself is, "An Expert." Because the people who say no to you about something most of the time are experts. Now, I am not saying that all experts are bad or don't know anything. The thing about experts is they see things within a box, a square, and they don't believe there could be something different. A different outcome, potential and so forth that can be so vastly different from what they know.

I have always said, the people that radically shake up an industry and change it are usually not the experts. It is an outsider that will transform the industry. When I was studying energy medicine and the various healing techniques that are out there, I remember the developer of a technique talk about how a chiropractor, doctor, nurse, etc., will not be as effective of a healer as someone who is not. He would go on to explain that, "Our minds know what the body is, what it can do and so forth and your learning will get in the way of you allowing for things to just be." I remember not liking that statement, but I started to understand why he was explaining it. I caught myself many times working on someone, looking at their energy field and seeing what comes up that is needed and it be something that chiropractically makes no sense whatsoever, but I would trust the process, perform what is needed and it was amazing on the results that would come out of it.

I had learned how many times my mind and my training has blocked me in ways from taking things to higher levels. I remember practicing a specific energetic chiropractic technique that would analyze the body to see what physical, chemical, mental/emotional, bioenergetic stressors may be affecting the body and can determine what part of the body is being overly stressed by this stressor. One time I was working on a man and I would keep getting uterus which needed work on. I would triple-check and keep checking to make sure this was accurate, which it was. I knew the person I was working on was a male who was born male so I knew it wasn't a transgender. Then, I let go of the mental block I was having and stated, there are so many things my mind would never understand when it comes to healing and I just trusted the process and performed the correction. The results afterwards, was a huge uplifting feeling for the practice member.

The Universe was trying to teach me to get out of my head. It definitely showed up often in my office, and when I started to see the pattern, I knew it was a sign. What I have learned in the past 7 years of practicing Chiropractic care is, the more I practice, the less I know. The less I know about the body, how it functions and how a specific adjustment, what it does to every reaction from the adjustment. I couldn't tell you that and no other person on this planet could. But, it doesn't stop me from learning and growing. It doesn't stop me from looking at things from different angles to see how I can grow as a practitioner and learn to be the best version I can be. This is why, when I started Chiropractic school, the stuff they were teaching was interesting, but it didn't have deep substance for me. It didn't hit home. It didn't move me in a way I thought it would.

This is when I started to study Universal Laws, Energy Medicine and wanted to understand the deeper fabrics of how the body functions on the deepest level possible. Even when I hit the deepest level possible, I would say, "Well, I understand at this level but that is all I have at this time." And I will revisit at another time to learn more and dive deeper because as we are infinite and there are infinite experiences for us to learn, grow, expand and evolve, so is it with knowledge and information. What we know now about the body, in 100 years, will be different. How about 1,000 years? 10,000 years? A million years? How much will we radically change and how much will the body radically change and evolve to? It's endless. This is why I wanted to start this chapter off by stating, we don't know everything and we never will.

When I was researching near-death experiments and reading blogs of mediums who channel someone who just crossed over, the common theme they say is, "I definitely am not all-knowing." What exists in the spiritual world happens in the physical world. The only way we grow, expand and evolve spiritually and physically is through constant growth and change. Constant seeking new information, knowledge but even more important: WISDOM. This is what propels us and drives us to expand and evolve like we were designed to. Remember law of creation #4 states, "The only thing that is constant is change, except the first 4 laws." As you dive into this world, you will start to see how true these laws of creation are. The beautiful part, these laws of creation exist in the spiritual world just as much as they do in the physical world. For what is above is also below.

When I was growing up, I used my mind to adapt to my lifestyle and what I mean by that is, I used knowledge to give me security. I felt that if I knew things and understood what people would share with me, I wouldn't feel lost, missing out or felt stupid in any way. I made sure I learned things, even things that didn't matter to me. I wanted to know so I could make sure, regardless of what was brought at me, I would have an understanding to it. Well, as time went on, I started to realize how knowledge of things didn't really bring happiness. I started to realize it actually made the world much more less colorful. Believing you know things, labels and information that was not uplifting to you and inspiring, it started to show it didn't matter much.

So, eventually, I started to let go of the information and start to realize that, I didn't need to know everything and that it was OK to be that way. I set myself up for failure every single time because the mind can only comprehend 0.001% of the information that exists. Only that much. The rest, the mind does not know. In this process, I started to focus more on the being and trust my intuition instead of believing I needed to know every single thing. It was amazing how life transformed and I became less stressed out. I didn't have as much anxiety or anxiousness. I started to have visions of surfing (FYI, I don't surf). And the message was, "Life is like a wave. You don't know how the wave is going to be or what may happen. You just jump on, ride it and let your inner guidance system guide you."

Have you ever had something or felt like you had to do something but had no intellect on the reason why? You were moved to do something? And it ended up being the right decision for you. It ended up being more than you could ever imagine? This is what happens when you live your life in flow and not get in the way. Because at the end of the day, the biggest battle will always be between you and you. No one else will interfere with your dreams and goals, except you. So why not start there?

The more I practice Chiropractic, the more I fall in love with what I do. The more amazement I receive every single day. The concepts of change and how the body heals, blows my mind every single time. Even when there are times I don't know if the person will achieve the results they desire because of all the accumulation of stress, wearing out the body and much more, it amazes me how the body figures things out. And even though, I understand the neurology and understanding of what I am doing, the effects that follow are the thing that keeps me in amazement. From a couple who have tried over 1 year to get pregnant and within 1-2 months, it happens with the help of Chiropractic. The beautiful thing is, the body is powerful beyond measure. Never doubt nature for it has ways and wisdom that is way beyond what we will ever understand. When we look at how much we truly know how the body works, we only know 1-10% most of what exists and what is performed in the body. We are barely touching the surface. This is why I love practicing chiropractic because I work on the 100%. I don't need to know all the inter fabrics on how the body heals, I just need to know where the interference is and remove that interference (subluxation) and allow the body to do the rest. Allow that intelligence that exists within you to do the rest.

When we get out of our minds and start to be guided by our hearts, we open the portal to infinite information. It is a portal that allows for us to tap into and gain insights, messages, wisdom, etc., that we need by the disposal of our own mind. Once we calm the mind, it allows for many of us to experience that inner voice that exists within us. I always say, "If you cannot hear the inner voice within, it is only because of the chatter above." It is the distractions, ways of life, excuses, stories, etc., that really get our minds busy. And then, we eventually feel like we have no time or not enough time in a day. But, if we focus on the things that can help calm your mind, that alone, will transform your life.

The more you feed into a system, the more the system grows. As we live in this information era, we are constantly feeding our brains all this information. Every day, we can jump on Google, and find out pretty much anything we want. As we continue to feed our brains with all the information, we start to teach it to be the guidance system of your life. You start to strengthen the lines of communication and will start to catch yourself using logic in all decision that you make.

I remember I was sitting at a restaurant with my wife, and in this restaurant, the tables are very close to one another. I remember two friends sitting next to us and one of them was talking about two job opportunities. They were looking at things from a very logical perspective. And this conversation must have gone on for an hour because every time I eavesdropped on the conversation, it ended up being the same one. But long story short, I remember at the end, the one girl who was talking about the different job opportunities she had in front of her, was very stressed out.

She was frustrated she couldn't figure it out nor could her friend help break it down enough logically to have helped her in the decision. One thing I noticed was, the girl who had the job opportunities broke things down so much, I was even amazed as I can be very heavily left brain dominant.
After they left, I started to talk to my wife and tell her I saw me in the girl next to me. I started to explain how I normally would be

about things and how I was once in her shoes. If logic couldn't figure it out, I would need time to show me. That was my old motto. But, what I learned in the meantime is completely different. Some times in life, you don't need to know everything. Logic will never give you all the answers of life. It cannot. Most of the answers reside outside of logic.

The top scientists in the world have come together and stated, "Based on their research, the Universe should not exist." Can you say that the Universe exists someway, somehow, outside the barriers of logic? The body you reside in surpasses logic every day. It is amazing what the body can do. The body is the most advanced technological system that has ever existed. For every single thing the body does, that is true technology if you ask me. The amount of computing power the brain has. The amount of power the heart has to pump blood throughout your entire body and never stops. How the immune system knows exactly where to go at the specific time. Or even deeper, how the body went from 2 cells into 40 trillion cells within 9 months and was organized in the position they needed to be, differentiated from liver cells, eye cells, brain cells, and much more. Logic cannot begin to understand these feats and concepts.

As I continued the discussion with my wife about the couple next to us, I asked myself, "How could have this process been easier, more enjoyable and what advice would I have given her?"

What I realized is, if she just focused on what makes her happy and what she would find fulfillment in, and don't worry about all the other details, it would have made the process so much easier. We always constantly focus on the details and focus on how it should be. In life, the best things that happen are the ones we don't know about. When we try to put our experiences in a box, it is only a matter of time before life starts to feel gray. You start to lose the zest of life. Instead, change your routine and keep things fresh.

Go face one of your fears. That will make you feel alive again. Facing your fears is a way to get energy flowing. When you face your fears, you get out of your comfort zone. Your brain will send all the signals in the world to stop you from doing something that is uncomfortable, dangerous or may cause damage/pain. But, when it is a fear that is like I have of rollercoasters or the fear of the open waters, when you face them, you break through the barriers and experience something new.

One of the fears I am going to face this year in 2018 is flying on a plane for over 8 hours. The longest I have ever been on a plane is 3 hours and 54 minutes. My wife and I plan on visiting Europe before we start to have kids and I have held myself back so many times about this. I let fear hold me back. I gave it power. And instead of focusing on the fear of flying for that long, I could have focused on the experience I would have while I am in Europe. When I was at ASU, there was an Italian program to where I could go to Italy for a semester, study Italian, a few different art classes and enjoy 3-4 months in Italy. It was going to cost an additional couple thousand for the program, and at first, I was very much interested.

But then, I let the fear of flying for that long push me away. I started to look for excuses and the one that I allowed to be the story to believe in was, those classes were not classes I needed to take for the most part and it would put me behind what I wanted to get done. It was a solid, logical story. I was trying to finish college in 3 years and that would have held me back a semester and I was not OK with that. Back then, I rushed through things to get it done. I guess the lessons I have learned through that process is, if I don't take time to smell the roses, I will have my entire life flash before my eyes. Thankfully, after 14 years, I have learned the art of smelling the roses. I am not a master of it yet, but what I have learned is, celebrate every victory of yours. Make sure, regardless of the size, big or small, celebrate it.

In the beginning of my career when we would hit records, I would be like great, let's work on the next. I would continue to say, we have more to do. When I graduated undergrad, I didn't even want to walk across the stage. I finished school in December and they don't have you walk until May. If it wasn't for a good friend of mine at that time who said, "Vic, you are not walking on stage for you. When you walk on stage, you are walking for your parents." When she said that, I stated I would be there.

What do you think happened after my graduation? I was surprised by something. It actually shocked me. In my mind, I thought, my biggest stepping stone is Chiropractic school and that is the final hoorah that I was going to do with schooling and that was the big goal. What I wasn't paying attention to and focusing on is all the small things that were leading up to the big thing. In life, the small things are what make up the big things. The big things never just happen. It is rare for that occasion. Everything is created from the small things. Don't believe me? Look at the basic foundation of what your body is made of. When you get down to it, your body is made up of atoms. How small are they? When you put them together in a specific formation and combine them multiple times, it adds up to your physical body. Pretty cool?

After my graduation, I saw my parents under the tent and I walked up and gave my mom a hug and a kiss. My father looked at me and said, "You did something I couldn't do." Now, I know you don't know my father, our family dynamics and all that stuff. My father doesn't really give compliments at all. He is more of a guy who sets the bar high for you and pushes you beyond that. For him to say those words, I literally felt like something shook my body and slightly froze. Immediately, tears hit my eyes and I looked up to drain them as fast as I could. I will never forget that moment. And if I never got out of my head, trusted my heart, and listened to my good friend, I would have never experienced that moment.

Never think we know all things. In order to stay young, keep your child-like energy, make sure in all that you create, focus on and desire in your life, have fun with it. Create the impossible because, at the end of the day, impossible just means, "I'm Possible." And you are possible to create the fullness and vastness of life if you let go, have faith and trust the process. It is trusting your heart, your soul's navigator, to guide you. Let your mind be cautious but don't let it be the leader. Let the heart lead the way.

This process takes time because due to being in a very informational era, we are starting to trust more and more with our minds rather than our hearts. And we are starting to create dilemmas for ourselves because of this. As I am writing this, the

US Stock Exchanges are finally experiencing a correction. In the stock markets, what goes up, must come down eventually, but what happens is, for the most part, you won't ever see the old lows anymore. It creates a new support or a new low. But, what are people doing when they see a 10% correction? You guessed it. They freak out. They worry if they should sell, or stay in the markets. The thing is, if you focus on your intuition and go with the flow, you will know if you truly should or not.

When shit hits the fan in your life, don't back down and start thinking logically. Instead, focus within and let your inner guidance system guide you. The beautiful thing is, when you start to use it more and more, the one thing it will always do is guide you to where you need to be. It will guide you to where your desires are or the experiences you need to grow, evolve and become more of who you desire to be.

In all the times I have trusted my heart, it has never let me down. There are times though, to be honest, when I thought I was trusting my heart, but in reality, it was my mind creating a way to fool me. You will know when it does that. Your mind will be racing. You will have FOMO (Fear Of Missing Out). FOMO exists when you become impatient or don't want to experience the pain. You feel there is a way to get rid or avoid the pain and you don't want to miss that ride. Here is something you can do to calm yourself and reconnect with your soul's navigator (your heart).

- ***Take 15 deep breaths. Breathe in as deep as you can and then just relax your body as the air comes out naturally without you pushing.***

- ***On your 15th breath, hold it for as long as you can***

- ***Once you are down, just take nice, slow deep breaths.***

- ***Ask yourself, "What is the story I am telling myself? What expectations do I have? What is my ideal outcome?"***

Once you ask those 3 questions, you will then, shift your focus and your energy on the story of what you desire rather than anything else.

And as always, what happens when you focus on something? You better believe it. Where your attention goes, energy flows. Where energy flows, realization grows. Once you shift your focus, you tell your eyes what to see. You tell it what to be aware of. And from there, you shift your focus one step at a time towards the story of what you desire.

I have done this so many times in the past that my current coach I have, Dr. Troy, has been amazing and really brought this back to life for me. It helps me see the bigger picture and then, instead of feeding something that will neither serve your greatest good nor what you truly desire, instead, focus on what is the desired story/outcome and make it happen.

This process you can do endlessly in all aspects of your life, but the key is, don't think you need to know all the answers or the steps or how it will happen. You have to let that go. Leave that to the Universe. There are times I will say, "And Universe, I leave this all up to you for you are the master organizer who will bring the people, the situations and the circumstances needed with divine timing for me to achieve, have or become what it is I desire."

Obviously, these changes are based upon what I am requesting for in the Universe Catalog of Human Being Experiences. And by the way, this thing does exist. You are the creator of the Catalog. And you create what you want to order based upon your thoughts, emotions and words! :)

So as we wrap up this chapter, I wanted to share with you the experiences that took me over 10 years to truly grasp and that is, "You don't need to know everything on how it will happen in your life. The more you let go of this, the more a fulfilled and inspired life you will live. The more curiosity and Aw you will experience."

Just create, declare to the Universe your wishes and be 100% certain, you know this has already been done. You already clicked the, "Submit Payment Button." The order has been processed and they are preparing your order and getting ready for shipping. Remember, our minds can neither perceive all the information nor perspectives that exist out there. Based upon what our brains can handle, we can only understand 0.001% of the information that exists in the world. Remember that the next time you feel you know something at 100%. It is a great way to humble the mind. I know it has for me.

Chapter 10

The Inevitable Truth

Here is the test to find whether your mission on earth is finished: If you're alive, it isn't.

Richard Bach

Seeing death as the end of life is like seeing the horizon as the end of the ocean.

David Searls

In this human life, we are all not getting out of here alive. There is such a limit to what we get to experience in this life. And the moment we come to realize that we will not last forever as the person you are today, it creates the moment to start living. For that, in order to lose the fear of death is the moment you start to truly experience living. It is as if when I was first creating my business, a business mentor of mine told me, "Don't look at the beginning of what you want to create, but instead, focus at the end in mind. Focus on your end game. When will you get out? What is your plan?"

For me at that time, it was weird to think of my end game of not practicing Chiropractic. I told him, "I would practice until I was in my grave." But as I let what he shared with me marinate, it was another experience life was sharing with me that taught me this principle. Death.

As you know from a few chapters ago, I talked about how I had a fear of death and an end to our soul. I thought there were levels we achieve and once those levels are done, we are not needed and we would merge back in with the Source and that was it. Why did I think this? I have no clue. Who told me this? I don't know. I felt that all things come to an end and nothing lasts forever, meant we don't either. But, it wasn't until I did some soul seeking to realize I was pointed in the wrong direction. Once I realized, what is my end game before my life is over? What do I want people to remember me as? What legacy do I want to leave? What do I want my kids to think of me? Grand kids? Great grand kids? What conversations would they have? What can I leave with them that would be a part of me?

When I started to let go of the fear of death, I started to live, and once I started to live, I started to focus on what I wanted to create for my family and what I wanted to leave to this world. Because each one of us, has a gift to give. Each one of us, has something great within ourselves to share with others that no one else can share. There is no such thing as someone is more gifted than another. We all are in this together and we all share common perspectives. When we blend together all the perspectives of the world, I believe that is when we can understand the true perspective of the human spectrum of emotions, experiences and life. The more we understand others, the more we can understand ourselves.

This chapter is to discuss death. A dark and gloomy subject but from this, we will appreciate the light so much more. My goal in this chapter is to truly put things together and create the highest level of inspiration I can for you. My goal is not motivation. Because when you need motivation, this is you doing something you don't want to do or dislike doing. Inspiration means in-spirit. It is the eternal flame from within that fuels what you desire, and no matter how much water is thrown on it, it will never cease to exist.

My main objective in this chapter is to have you start living your life every day, like it is your last day. When we get caught up in the human emotions of things, we start to lose our sights on the big picture of life. We start to blur the lines as I like to say. When was the last time you were caught up in your emotions and when time had passed on, you looked back saying, "I forgot the bigger purpose behind things." We all have been there. There are many numerous times in my life when I let my emotions get the best of me. Or when I would continue in an argument that pulled away from the main point or reason of the argument in the first place. Ever had an argument to where halfway into it, you completely forgot why you were arguing in the first place? I've been there many times before.

The truth is, every single thing that has existed in the physical world, has a timeframe stamped on it. It has its own internal stop clock. It has a beginning and an end. When we look at animals, humans, plants, trees, etc. They all have a beginning and an end. When we look at planets, stars, galaxies, universes, etc., they all have a beginning and an end. All physical things don't last forever. But the essence of who you are does. The essence of who you are transcends all time and space. As we explained in chapter 1, you are endless, timeless and eternal. In the view of your soul, this life is within a blink of an eye. The time frame is very short. We don't have the opportunity to live 1,000 years on this planet. We get 80-100 years if we are lucky enough to experience what this world has to offer and how it helped us re-discover who we are, expand and evolve into the person we desired in this lifetime. At the same time, your soul expands and evolves as your physical self does also.

So, when our time is so limited, is it truly worth doing the things you don't like to do? Is it worth busting your ass 12-16 hours a day to make ends meet, to trade that time to miss out on time with your family? To miss out on time with your family growing up?

I know how it is to be raised in a family where they are making ends meet. I grew up in a blue collar family where my dad had 2 jobs and my mom had 3 part-time jobs to just make ends meet. I am forever grateful for everything they sacrificed to give me the life I had. I will never forget that and will forever be in debt for their love and support. But the thing it taught me was, I didn't want to have to be away from my family, to provide financially but miss out on them growing up. I didn't want to not see my kids at days and sometimes weeks at a time. I will never forget that I almost didn't see my dad for an entire month. He was working overtime at his main job and then, trying to keep up with his carpet business at the same time. Some may not believe this, but when my dad worked 3p-11p and I would get home at 2:45pm when he had already left, it happened easily.

This brought up a question to me, and it was experiencing two good friends and my grandfather pass on. These experiences taught me a common lesson. If you had only 24 hours left to live, what would you do? How would you spend your time? Would you continue to do the same things you do on a daily basis? Would you spend all that time watching TV? The News? Reading a book? What would you do if you only had 24 hours left to live?

When I truly started looking at my life and letting this be the forefront of thought, I started to realize that, most of the things I worry about, most of the things I do, didn't matter. What mattered to me were two things. Spending time with close friends/family and sharing with the world anything I can about inspiring their lives to bring more of their light upon this world. That was all that came to mind. So, I had to be real with myself and look at my life and say, what didn't suit what I would do in the last 24 hours would not be a priority to me no more.

From that moment on, I made sure I spend every night with my wife, even if it is 30 minutes, just to spend time, connect and enjoy our time together in whichever way she desires. I would make sure I connect with friends who are my good friends that would have my back regardless of anything. I would make sure I always have a solid relationship with my parents and let them know I love them. You never know how long your parents will last on this planet. From there, it inspired me to start writing my book that you are reading now. I actually have a goal to write 30+ books in my lifetime, if I am destined to. Wayne Dyer was a mentor to me and I was amazed on the amount of books he wrote and the influence he had and the deep radical changes he made in people's lives. I never met the man, but he helped inspire my life and I want to pay it forward.

I want to know, when I do have my last 24 hours left on this planet as Victor Manzo Jr., I want to make sure I am on empty. I want to make sure, I have nothing left to give. I want to make sure that I gave it my all and that I was truly a blessing to have on this planet. At the end of the day, this is what inspires me and drives me. Because, in my last 24 hours, I want to enjoy it with my family and make sure I have done all I can for humanity and this planet. Everything we do in this life, affects every other person in some way, shape or form.

The moment you let your light shine, you allow the possibility for others to do the same. You give them the opportunity to do just that as of which you did. Everything we do in this lifetime, echoes into eternity and it is shared upon one another. Every single thing that happens in each human's life is shared upon the human collective consciousness. We are all inputting experiences into this consciousness and what we do in our lives, is uploaded into the human collective. Everything we do also has a ripple effect upon the Universe. This is how powerful you are.

So, for us to play out big, to let our light shine, and to truly appreciate the power we have within, is a way to live a fulfilled and inspired life not only for yourself, but also give the opportunity for others to do the same thing.

The bitterest tears shed over graves, are for words left unsaid and deeds left undone.

Harriet Beecher Stowe

I have learned over time that the richest place in the world is not the physical wealth that exists in this world but in the graveyards of lost ideas, dreams and deeds left undone or never unleashed. The graveyard is a place where many dreams and wishes were unsaid, undone and unfulfilled. The potential of what that would have been done for humanity, for their own experience and for their own legacy is priceless and something we will never know.

If you are here right now, you have a purpose. You are here for a reason. The Universe does not waste energy. Everything is always used and put to a purpose. It is the same thing of the human body. The body will recycle up as much as it can of energy to be as energy efficient as possible. I remember my physiology teacher was talking to us about the energy efficiency of our bodies and compared it to a gallon of gasoline. He stated if a car was as efficient with energy as our bodies our, one gallon would last us approximately 1,000 miles or more. That is how efficient our bodies are at conserving energy. The Universe is the same. All things will be recycled and utilized in some shape or form.

Another lesson the body taught me about the Universe. When a cell is about to die, it will go into a big shake and explode giving itself upon the rest of the cells. It shares all that it has within to other cells to use and consume for their needs.

The Universe does the exact same thing. When a star explodes, all the dust, materials and so forth, will soon, one day, be recycled and used up by the Universe to start new life. This is an endless cycle that occurs and life will never be left unused.

This is why everything has a reason for its existence or else, it wouldn't be here. If you are still alive, you have a reason for your existence. The question is, "What is it? Why are you still here?"

Ask yourself the question, "Why do I wake up every morning? What is the drive for me to get up?"

When I ask these questions, I will normally hear things like, "Because I have to work." "The bills need to be paid." "The kids need to go to school." Etc.

But in reality, what is the deeper reason why? There is a purpose to why we wake up and get on with our day? We didn't do all this work as a soul to come into this small little body to have a human being experience to just wake up every morning and go to work and take the kids to school. You came here for something greater. If you know what it is, great. If not, here are some questions to ask yourself.

If you had 24 hours left to live, what would you do? How different would it be from your life now?

If money was no objective and you knew you would not fail, what would you like to do in this lifetime?

These two questions transformed my reality. It shifted my perspective. It started to create a fulfilled life for me. And the thing that I always keep in focus is, when I wake up, I say, "I have another 24 hours to create an experience, what shall I experience today?" And the other is, "If this is my last 24 hours, how do I want to maximize it to the fullest?"

As we get older, they say, you start to care less about things and come into yourself more. You don't worry about the little nuances of life. Like for me, when I was a teenager, it was all about looking good, wearing the right clothes, etc. I always wanted to look good always, especially when I hung out with friends. Speed forward 16 years and I am the total opposite. I can care less of how I look. As long as I am comfortable, that is all that matters. Don't get me wrong, when the opportunity arises to get dressed up in a suit, I make sure I let my Italian side come out and look good. But other than that, it is not a necessity for me. And I believe with life, you do the same thing with other things.

One thing I have been told and taught is to never hold a grudge with anyone. Always let go and forgive. Because when you hold a grudge, when you are angry at someone, what you really are doing is, drinking the poison and hoping they get hurt from it. It is like grabbing a hot coal and hoping they burn from it. Who gets hurt in the end? Who suffers? It is not the person you are holding a grudge to, but the person who holds the grudge which is YOU.

Forgiveness is truly another word for understanding. When someone does something wrong to you, hurts you, betrays you, causes harm, why shift our mindset into a victim? Why do we need to forgive in the first place? What is the purpose of forgiveness?

Since forgiving myself for my shortcomings in all that I do is tough because I am so hard on myself but then again, who isn't? I remember in a meditation I received this long message about forgiveness. It started out with a little voice saying, "Forgiveness does not exist and it is not needed." I was shocked to hear this. I am like, "Forgiveness is always needed. We must apologize for when we have a mistake or a shortcoming in life." And the voice started to explain why.

"At the viewpoint of where I am, you will realize that every single person is doing the best they can with the information and resources they have. If you went through every single experience that they have gone through, you would do the same thing. There is no difference between each of us. Forgiving someone for doing their best is not ideal nor makes much sense. No one could ever judge an individual's effort and each human being on this planet is giving 100% effort every single day, regardless of what anyone else thinks. Instead, when someone does something to hurt you, upset, you, anger you, etc., come from the vantage point of understanding. Put 100% effort into understanding that in some unique way, they are doing the best they can. And as a fellow brother/sister in the human race, our job is to help create perspective and clarity for them and when two people come from a place of understanding, love blossoms each and every time."

If you don't think so, think about the last big argument you had with a significant other, friend or family member and how things were when you finally came to an understanding. Did you appreciate each other less or more? Did you love less or more?

If you truly came from an understanding place, it is then, you experience love and allow for love to flow. How do you become more understanding? Focus on it. Never forget, your focus is what creates your reality. The things you focus on things within a daily basis, is what is slowly creating the fabrics to your reality.

Every one of you waking up every single day, don't say to yourself, "I want to live less than my potential. I want to be less than 100%." I have done 1,000s of workshops and speaking events and when I ask, "How many of you want to experience 100% health?" I never met someone who said less than that. But yet, majority of people don't do the things they know to do.

Then when you look at your life and focus on where you are at this exact moment, have you given 100% your effort? Have you done all that you are capable of in living a fully inspired life? Achieving your goals? Achieving your dreams?

Most of the time, the answer is NO. We can always do more and we will always be able to do better. The real thing you have to be with yourself is to be 100% honest if you did the work. Because everything I have shared in this book with you is how this game called, "Life," works and if you truly focus on the reality, the vision, the life you want to create, if you give 100% your attention and focus to, it is IMPOSSIBLE for it to not be attracted into your world. It is IMPOSSIBLE. The only reason why things are not happening to you is because you are allowing distractions to the things that you are focusing on. Life is going to throw bullshit at you in every direction. And the moment you start to feel burnt out, overwhelmed, in a rut, that is because you are paying more attention to the distractions than you are to your vision.

The truth is, there are three guarantees in life: death, taxes and distractions. I say this because life is constantly going to challenge you and mold you. It will create circumstances for you to overcome. It will constantly send challenges your way to test where you are and help you achieve the characteristics you desire to evolve into who you want to be. But regardless of your stories of the reasons why you are not where you desire to be, or creating excuses why you don't have time to get something done, take time for yourself, work out, eat right, etc., instead, get back to your focus and stop giving the excuses power over your desires.

I know I have done this numerous of times in my life and I know this probably has happened to you. It was a long day and you've been saying you want to get up early to get work done and continue to move forward in life. You continue to focus on getting up early and feel inspired to. But, when the morning comes, you are a different person than who you were 6-8 hours ago. What you end up doing is, hitting the snooze button 1, 2, 3, 4… times and don't wake up like you wanted to, don't achieve the things you wanted to get done and don't start on the solid footing you stated you would. What happened from the night before until that morning that didn't have you wake up as you stated you would?

For me, it was the excuses I told myself. It was the stories I bought into. It was the distractions of where I was at that moment that I allowed to take over me. I have had this battle go on and off from time to time. And when I start to catch myself drifting away from my focus, I re-center, regroup and remember my WHY of what I am doing. I remember the purpose of why I am doing what I am doing. I reconnect with myself and my source to allow me to get back being focused on the vision and the why. I visualize that when I leave this world, I want to make sure I am on empty. I don't want to have anything left that I may have kept within. I want to know that, when my life review happens, I look at my life and say, "Man, I gave it my all. I gave it 100%."

Don't let these little distractions and B.S. stories pull you away from your vision. Don't let the excuses come in. Catch yourself making excuses because if you are not experiencing the life you desire, it is because you are creating excuses to not do it. You are not doing the work. You are not being focused on what it is you desire. Get rid of the excuses and the stories. Hell, create a story that inspires you and helps you stay on track. To be honest, I am not a morning person. I dislike getting up early. I rather sleep in. But, I had to change this story around in order to start to like getting up early. I started to shift my focus on, not the things I dislike, but rather, what do I like. Why do I get up around 3:45a - 4:45a most mornings? Because by the time 8am - 9am rolls around, I have already done most of my work for the day and that allows for me to focus on other things during lunch and then I am able to relax in the evenings with my family and unwind for the night. This is the purpose behind why I get up early.

Again, if you change your focus on whatever it is, you will change your reality. Just like I changed my focus on finding what it is I liked about getting up early in the mornings and just focused on that.

Another guidance to follow that has become much truth in the making. Focus on doing the small things each and every day of your life. Don't focus so much on doing big things. The big things don't matter. What truly matters is the small things because when you add up the small things, they will become big things. A marathon is started with your first step. Daily growth in inches, will eventually one day, be a mile. It is the things you do on a consistent basis that will create the reality you choose to experience. All you need to do is focus and give it your all. And your all means, giving 100% your effort every single day. This is the formula to finishing your life on E (empty).

So, what is it in your life you want to maximize? What area? Your health? Mindset? Spirituality? Relationships? Career? Start up a business? Finance?

All of these things can transform and become what you choose to experience. The question comes down to, how much are you going to focus on the vision and what is your game plan when you become distracted? How will you rebound back to focus on your vision? What do you have that will help anchor you?

I know for me, the visualization is seeing myself in my last day, knowing that I finished on E and when I do that, I gave this world all that I was able to give. I gave to my family which in the long run, ends up continuing my legacy forward and helping my family and the human race family, have the same opportunity to do the same. This is the level of urgency you want to play with in your life. You only have one life and this life is short. So don't spoil the time you have on meaningless things that do not give back to you. Don't spoil your time on the people that don't help challenge you and inspire you. Don't spoil your time on what people have to say or what their opinions are of what you want to do with your life.

What you will start to realize is, when you start to truly follow your purpose and what you want to achieve in this world, many friends and family will not be around as much. You won't have the same amount of friendships you used to have at one time. As your values and focus change, most of the time, the people you associate with change. It is the law of association.

I remember when I decided to go to Arizona State University, and in the town I was growing up in, that was not common. Most of the kids would go to Universities or Colleges nearby. Rarely did we hear about someone moving away, especially a 3.5 hour flight away. But I did that. I wanted something different for myself and I wanted to experience a different life than what I had. I felt there was more out there. Before I left, I had tons of friends. But, within 1 year, the tons of friends dwindled down to about 10 close friends. And as time went on, I changed, I kept seeking for more and focusing on my goals and visions, that my group of friends went down even more. This was a time in my life when I realized what my dad told me for years. He would tell me while looking at his hand, "If you can count the amount of good friends to the fingers you have in one hand, considered yourself lucky." As I have gotten older, I started to see how this is true. I have a couple very close and personal friends who I consider my brothers. We are always celebrating our victories, helping each other grow, sharing ideas and always looking out for the best in each of us. There is no competition. All it is, is about having fun, achieving our dreams and living life to the fullest. We all want to end up being on E when it comes time for our crossing over.

My question is, how much do you want to end up on E when it comes time for you to cross over?

I want you to write out a list of things that you want to achieve in your life. Map out the things that you truly want to accomplish and write it all out. From there, you take your time to understand, how much are you committed to achieving? Level it from 1-10, 1 being not much and 10 being, all in.

Make this grade sheet in your life so you can take the time to figure this out. If you don't want to, visit my website at https://bit.ly/2GIv738 and you will find this under, "How to Live to E Worksheet."

Fill this out and truly focus on what it is you want to create from your life. Know that you don't have forever, but if you start now, with the small things, focus on who you choose to be and then from there, focus on the action steps you can take at this time to make it happen.

From there, once you decide, a part of your brain will shift gears for you and help you make sure you focus on that. But you have to choose and then, focus on this with all your might and don't let the distractions get to you.

I sometimes say, "It is a do or die mentality." The Do-Die mentality basically means this and don't mind the extreme of this: If someone put a gun to your head and told you, you either get your goals done or you're done, how much would that help you get your shit done?" I bet every one of you would say, "I would make it happen someway, somehow." It is that determination, that mentality to what creates the reality of your dreams.

For me in my life, when it comes to eating clean, working out, spending time with my relationship with self, connecting with my source, connecting with my wife and family, these are the things that are do or die. I do them, or else I start dying within. No one is holding a gun to me, but what I do know is, every day, you are either expanding in the areas of your life or you are shrinking, but it is never staying still or doing both. It is one or the other. So, when you add a little fuel to the fire each and every time, you slowly are creating a fire that will continue to burn and grow. What happens when you don't fuel the fire?

It gets smaller and smaller until you continue with the fuel. Even too much fuel is not a good thing. This is why simple addition to fuel each and every day is the key to creating the life you desire. But make sure you are utilizing the keys we talked about in this book and in this chapter to help you create a life so that, when you come to the End, you are on E.

Chapter 11

Creating An Inspired and Fulfilled Life

"You are ready and able to do beautiful things in this world, and as you walk through those doors today, you will only have two choices: love or fear. Choose love, and don't ever let fear turn you against your playful heart."

"It's better to FAIL at what you LOVE than to FAIL at what you DON'T."

Jim Carrey

A solid truth is, "You already possess everything within." All the resources that you need to achieve your dreams, transform your life, change course, expand your life even more, and so forth, all exist within you. As I work with clients, have on my online programs and different programs we offer at Empower Your Reality, we are not teaching you anything really new. What we are doing, is helping you re-discover what you already have. This entire book is designed to help you discover who you really are, how to play in the game called, "Life," and create the best life you could ever imagine. Truth be told, if you can imagine it, it is possible. And as long as something is possible, the Universe can figure out a way to create the experience you have chosen.

So, as we wrap up this book in this last chapter, know that, when you want to create something in your life, you first, must focus on it because when you focus on something, it is then, you are putting your source energy into things and your source energy, is what gives life to all things. Then from there, keep your focus on it but don't worry about how the Universe will provide or in which way it will happen. Just keep your focus on what you desire and make sure your words, the stories you tell yourself, the emotions you invite with the process, never go against what your vision is.

For example, I stated earlier I want to write over 30 books in my life. I feel like I have so much to share and even though, it is just my perspective and experiences on things, I know there is someone out there that can benefit from it. But, my mind will come in and try to give me doubt. I am 34 years old, writing my first book, and if I want to write 30 books in my career, I would have to write 1 book a year on average and I will be 64. That is a ton of writing, especially the work I had to do in writing this book. But, if let go of the stories, excuses and the bullshit that will distract me from the vision and just say, I am writing those 30 books regardless and the Universe will provide, it will happen. Be certain with what you state to the Universe without having any doubt. Don't let doubt and fear get in the way; they are the things that will hold you back most in life.

But more importantly, don't let the people who are closest to you hold you back from your dreams. Unfortunately, the people closest to you usually will hold your dreams back. They will say things like, "That cannot work. Look at the economy. There are no jobs. etc." There are endless stories and statements that they will say. And for most, it is not their fault and it is not that they don't want to see you succeed or at least most of them. It is their fears that are projecting upon you. It is what limits them to what may limit you. It is called, "The Lobster Effect." What the lobster effect is, you can have 3 lobsters in tank. One of the lobsters says, I am done with this life in this tank, I am going to see what else exists for me. As it starts to attempt to get out of the tank, the other two lobsters will work together to keep the lobster from getting out of the tank. For what reason they do this, I have no clue, but what I do know is, fear must hold them back. They don't want to allow for someone to leave for their life would change and be different. So, as much as that lobster struggles to get out of the tank, the other two will work as hard as they can to keep it in there.

Breaking through barriers in your life is the exact same process. You have to put enough energy into the concept and not allow for things to get in the way. If you allow for stories, excuses or even fear get in the way, it will kill your dreams and kill the life you choose to experience.

Fear is primarily a mental construct created by your mind to keep you out of danger. Fear is not something that exists. There are some real fears in life but majority of them are made up. For example, I have a deathly fear of sharks or open water. Now, if you put me on a big lake, different story. But if you put me on the ocean, I will freak out. Why? I have no clue. But what I have learned is, when I face my fears and when it's over, I am usually like, "Why did I waste so much energy on that fear and keep it alive?"

When I was 15 years old, I faced a fear that I had of roller coasters. And my motto is, "I go big or I go home." What ended up happening is, I chose the biggest rollercoaster at that time, "The Raging Bull," at Great America. This thing had a 200 foot drop and then another 150 foot drop and bunch of other things included in this ride. I said to myself, "I am going to face this fear."

After that first 200 foot drop was over and I was inches away from a heart attack, I felt freedom and when the next 150 foot drop came, I was not even bothered. I actually looked forward to the feeling. All the other rollercoasters I went on that day, didn't bother me as much and I was blown away by how much I didn't mind them. I will say, I don't like rollercoasters that much. Not because of the fear anymore but more because the thrill doesn't really give me that excitement like many people do. But I can say I did it. :)

The key to life is to figure out a way to allow for your light to shine and I personally believe it is drowning the noise around you and just focusing on you. Focus on what you want to experience in your life and only think of your feelings. Because when this life is all said and done, it won't matter how many fancy cars you have, the square footage of your home or if you have a private jet or not. What will truly matter is what is left within your heart. What you did for others and yourself is all that will carry on with you. This is worth more than any currency that will ever exist on any planet. What are the things you can do to empower others or be that beacon of light for someone?

As one of my spiritual teachers taught me. She said, "If you help one person, shift their life and help them realize the power they have within, you have made a massive difference in the world. You help create a ripple effect." All it takes is one person to shine their light and it will help others illuminate their own.

Now, as you have learned from this book, the key of everything I shared with you wasn't only to help you understand the laws of life, but also how to truly emanate your light upon this world. How can you help make this world brighter? The more you live by your demands, your wishes, your dreams, the more you illuminate this world because it allows for you to shine your light bright. That is the biggest concept of my book and the main goal.

Throughout each chapter, I hope it created dialogue with you. I hope it had you ask yourself questions and help create awareness. The concept of this book and the things I shared in each chapter truly are just to give you the concepts of what you focus on, gives energy/life to which you focus on. I know, deep down, there are two things people want to be. Happy and Healthy. I have asked this question many times in different ways and I would always get happy and healthy. Well, if we were truly happy, why is America becoming more and more depressed? Why are more and more people on anti-depressants? Obviously, we are missing something and I believe it is living the dreams of others instead of living our own.

I wasn't taught how to live for myself and my dreams. I was taught growing up that you don't want to hurt anyone's feelings and you don't want to offend or disrespect anyone. The happiness of another is worth more value than my own happiness. And growing up, when I would want to do what I wanted to do, I would be reprimanded for doing the things that I didn't follow. I was a stubborn kid but I loved dancing in life to the beat of my own drum. And eventually, over time, I started to learn this lesson.

I will not say it was easy to stand up for what I desired. To focus and declare what I like to do that makes me happy. In my relationship, my wife has been great with this. She will ask me, "What do you want to do to be happy?" And I will ask, "What do you want to do?" And she will throw it back at me before she answers.

You are the only person that will defend and create the life that you desire. No one can do it for you. It is you and only you. You are the creator of your dreams and the destroyer of them. It is all about what you feed and what you give into that will make the difference of your reality.

Since focus was the main topic of this book and always referencing back to it, I wanted to share with you something that I know has worked for me as I developed my own way of helping me stay focused, laser focused and allowed to create the life of my dreams.
You will hear many things to help you stay focused and be committed to something. It can be meditation, breath work, cryotherapy, aromatherapy, herbs, supplements, working out, food, chiropractic, acupuncture, qi gong, tai chi, journaling, writing, gratitude, prayer, etc. I can go on and on about what people state is what helps them stay calm and focused on the prize.

The thing I want to share with you is find what works for you. Don't allow others to tell you what works. Instead, learn from someone and then develop your own blueprint that helps you stay centered, calm, balanced and focused on your vision.

When I first started Chiropractic school, I remember the professors telling us we would have to spend 3 hours studying a day in order to obtain all the information we were learning and to do well on the exams. Since it was my first trimester and my first experience in Chiropractic school, I did whatever people were saying to do. Most people were studying in the library and I would join. We would study from 4-7pm and sometimes even later.
As I did this for the first trimester, I started to realize how I was feeling burnt out and overwhelmed. I did well on my first trimester where I had all A's and one B. I was proud of that, but at the same token, I couldn't see myself continuing doing this for another 8

more trimesters. So, instead, when the 2nd trimester came around, I started to change the way I studied that I felt worked best for me.

What I ended up finding out was, if I see things into the big picture of all the stuff we were learning, it would shorten my time to where I only needed to study 1-2 hours for an exam. As I started to do this, I started to realize how, my grades dipped a bit, but retaining the information I was able to retain the information longer.

If I had not jumped outside the norm and attempt to discover what works for me, who knows how my experience in Chiropractic school would have been. But what I do know is, discovering my path on studying, is what allowed for me to take as many seminars as I did while I was in school and not be extremely burnt out from all the studying and sitting for 8-12 hours a day.

My question to you is, "What are the things you are doing because everyone else is doing that in a particular way or are you going along life based upon what you were taught as the way of life? Have you developed your own path? Are you living your life at the way you desire to live?"

The thing about life is, no one really knows anything to be 100% truth or being 100% right. Not one single soul on this planet. And many of you may say, "Jesus or Buddha, Krishna knew everything." The truth is, these Avatars that walked our planet, they knew the connection to source. They knew how the world is and how everything flowed. They knew that we were God and God is us. They were the mirror of who we really are and what our potential is. Jesus himself said, "You will do great works beyond what I have done." I am paraphrasing the scripture, but the key thing is, Jesus's disciples did carry on what Jesus stated, but when he said we would do greater work than him, he meant all of us. Because outside this bubble that we live called, "the human body." Within that bubble truly is the same stuff. We all have a heart, a lung, a liver, a brain, etc. We all experience the same exact emotions: anger, frustration, happiness, joy, bliss, peace, serenity, etc. The only difference we have when it comes to emotions is how we express our emotions. Some people when they get angry, shut down. Some become very verbal. Some get physical. All different acts. None are right nor are they wrong. They are the way the person expresses their nature. There is always a better way, and I am a big component of learning better ways to manage, handle and understand the emotions I face and I believe everyone else is too.

But, the beautiful thing is, when I say the Universe is working FOR you, not AGAINST you, to be honest, I have no clue for that to be true. I have no concrete evidence. Based upon meditations, research and so forth, I believe that everything that happens in your life is for a reason. And that reason is designed to help you expand and evolve. It is the one thing I know for certain. This life is designed by you, for you, for your highest good, to expand and evolve.

But at the end of the day, the only truth is the one you set the stage for. The only truth is the one that you believe in to be true for you. Because when this is all over, you will discover you are your own universe. You create your own laws within your universe. You have your own experiences and much more. You are a universe who is everlasting, expanding and evolving into whatever you desire. For it has and always will be up to you. God gave us a blessing of life and allows for us to go out and experience life in all its forms. That is all was asked upon us. The rest is up to us.

Years ago, I was reading a book that shifted my entire consciousness of money. Actually, my entire experience of life. In Wallace Wattle's book, "The Science of Getting Rich," he made a statement in there that said, "Why would God want to experience less than what is optimal? Why would God want to minimize your experiences of life?" Don't you think God wants you to experience all this life has to offer? You cannot experience all the things this human life has to offer as we discussed earlier. It takes many lifetimes, 1,000s of lifetimes to grasp the understanding and experiences of being human. I mean, think about it. How many facets are there to being human? Add in culture, eras, villages, civilizations, human collective consciousness at that time and much more. This human being experience is endless within itself.

So, what I grasped from the book overall is that in order to fulfill my life, is helping God fulfill Itself. If I experience all there is to experience in this life, God will experience all that can be experienced through me in this life. And since the book was about money, it talked about how God would want you to be rich. It doesn't want you to be poor. When you have money, it creates more opportunities to experience this life. Notice he didn't say happiness. He said, "Create opportunities for living your life." That really is what money is all about. It creates opportunities and research even shows after a specific point of how much money you make, it doesn't change much after that point.

So, through this book, on all that you have learned and will apply in your life, how can you create more opportunities in your life that will ultimately, allow for God to experience through you?

The life you are living is a co-creation with the Prime Creator (God). You are able to create lives, go out and live your own, create your own path, and in the end, God gets to experience that lifetime and experience more of Itself. How cool is that?

This is why, I have devoted my life to raising the consciousness of every single human being I come in contact with. My goal is to help them realize the amazing light they already are. You are unbelievably amazing. You are one of a kind. Don't let anyone tell you something different. God did not create two of the same for a purpose that is beyond the words I can express. You were created out of a need, not a want. Don't ever forget that.

Look into your life and see where you want to create more fulfillment, more inspiration and utilize the principles that we shared in this book to be a guide for you. This entire book was meant to be a guide. It is not something you do A, B, C, D, etc., to get these results: A, B, C, D, etc. This was meant to be an evaluation tool and be an opportunity for you to start to realize how to take full control of your life and what the methods to do such a thing are.

I have tested throughout the past 10+ years, all these methods I have shared within this book and know for them to be true. I have read many books, studied many individuals, taken many courses, workshops, and listened to many podcasts to understand the depths of what I shared with you. I wanted to know it and feel it. I wanted to come to a realization of knowing and feeling within that, I am the creator, the writer, the author, the producer, the actor, the screenwriter, the everything of all things within my life. And whenever I wanted to make a change, I can do so within a second and then, just focus on that change and see it materialize into my life.

Remember, when you visualize, don't worry about how it will happen or the steps to making it happen. The key thing is to just make sure you stick your focus on the vision and know the rest is taken care of for you. Why? Because the Universe works FOR you, not AGAINST you. It will always bring your highest good for why would God not want to experience what you are wanting to experience?

One of the things you never want to do is do the things that will create acceptance for others. If you do, you will be invisible to all people and to the world. Never allow for yourself to worry about pleasing another human being to sacrifice your dreams, your wishes or a life you desire to experience.

I live by two rules in life. Two rules that govern me in all that I do. It is the two things that I do not stand for. These two things are: Never suppress anyone and don't kill anyone. I think these two things are the same thing. One actually holds someone down in a way that puts a death to their voice while the other ends the person's life.

Never let anyone suppress or interfere with your dreams, your voice, your will, your desire. Let that shit shine bright. Let yourself shine bright. Once you start to do this work, you will start to realize the beauty of who you are and then will see all the amazing beauty around you. The more you appreciate yourself, the more you appreciate others and the world you experience, which is truly amazing.

> "I am very serious about no alcohol and no drugs. Life is too beautiful."
>
> *Jim Carrey*

Life truly is a beautiful process, but as you have discovered, no matter what you face in life, it is all about your perspective, what you focus on, that will truly determine if life is absolutely amazing or the total opposite. You have the power to experience whatever it is you desire.

Just stay committed to what you want to experience and have the faith to know it will happen. And this faith is not religious by any means. When I say faith, I mean knowing deep within that it has already been done. It is like ordering something from Amazon and you know it will be at your house on the same day, next day or 2-day shipping. It is like ordering a movie on-demand, and once you click "buy," you know it is yours to experience. It is like wanting to listen to country music, so you know if you switch the tuner to the station 99.5 (in Chicago), you know you will experience country music. It is having faith like this that will sink in and truly help you achieve all the greatness that lies ahead of you.

I want to thank you for reading this book. I hope it enlightens your life as much as the stories, wisdom, experiences and knowledge have enlightened mine. We are all in this game called, "Life," together. The more we share with others, the more we live towards the calling of our own heart, the more enriched the life we experience and allow for others to do the same thing.

Namaste!
The light (soul) within me, honors and appreciates the light (soul) within you!

ABOUT THE AUTHOR

Dr. Victor Manzo Jr., is the co-founder of The Wellness Path and founder of Empower Your Reality. He is the creator and host of *Wellness Smart Radio* and *The Mindful Experiment* podcasts. Dr. Vic is a family wellness and pediatric chiropractor, Reiki Master and Trainer and advocate for humanity's growth and expansion in consciousness. Dr. Vic lives in the suburbs of Chicago.

CONNECT WITH DR. VIC

Website: www.EmpowerYourReality.com
Chiropractic Website: www.VisitTheWellnessPath.com

Facebook……………….../DrVicManzo
Instagram……………….../DrVicManzo
YouTube……………….https://bit.ly/2wvGlfU
Twitter…………………/DrVic21
Linkedin………………./DrManzo
SnapChat………………./DrVic21

www.ingramcontent.com/pod-product-compliance
Lightning Source LLC
Chambersburg PA
CBHW062216080426
42734CB00010B/1916